ᴅISCOVERING UPWELL

By
William P ⁚
ISBN 978-0-95⸱

GW00645045

Local history and photographic illustrations

SCENES - BUILDINGS- EVENTS - VILLAGE PEOPLE- TALES and ILLUSTRATIONS

First published November 2012

Published by
CARRILLSON PUBLICATIONS
WWW.CARRILLSON.CO.UK

Printed by
Newprint & Design Ltd

All rights reserved. No part of this book maybe reproduced or transmitted in any form or by any means, electronic or mechanical including photocopying, recording or by any information storage and retrieval system without permission in writing from the publisher.

Contains: Approximately 200 illustrations 224 pages and over 50,000 words

ACKNOWLEDGEMENT

I am profoundly grateful to those who have contributed to the making of this book. Unfortunately, there are a number of them who are unable to share the completion with us. There are perhaps many people better qualified than me who might have produced a document about the village history; in fact there are a few that did. Dr. Montgomery, The Reverend Richard Jeans and George Smith have contributed much over the years; their work is very much valued and appreciated.

My gratitude is extended to the following and I sincerely apologise to those I may have overlooked.
<u>Sally Harrison, Christopher Ransome</u>
<u>Graeme and Silvia Lawson</u>

Dick Francis, Oliver & Michael Barrowclough, Bridget Holmes, Muriel Byton, Irene Overland, Mr & Mrs Patrick Floyd, Gerry Moore (cycle historian of Brandon), Philip Doubleday, the late Dr. Sandy Greer, Dr. Paul Millard, the late Hugh Brown, Ray & Jan Wicks- Etcetera, Joy & Brian Tweed, Rita & Arthur Cuss, Graham & Barbara Seaton, the Stittle family, David Horn, John Francis, Bill & Mary Williamson, Tony Rivett, Don & Anne Frusher, Richard Bristow (Norfolk Pubs), Graham & Jean Tidmas, Gerald Harnwell, Thelma Butcher, the late Jack Plumb, Peggy Foster, the late Lillian Heanes and family (custodians of The Charles Chapman/Dr Tubbs collection), Ivor Pollington, Pauline Organ (Gilbertine Soc) Peter Dorling, Mr & Mrs G Melton. Mr & Mrs M Pope, Mr N Pope, Mrs (Marg) Barrett, Mr & Mrs Mick Overland, Malcolm (Mally) Pope, Mick Winters, David Grey, Stephen Calton, Mrs Derek Sutton, Hazel Hancock, Graham & Jean Tidmas, Jack Francis, Dr Paul Williams, Mike Greenbank, Elgoods Brewery, Robert Bell, Wisbech and fenland Museum & the Lilian Ream col. Alison Adamson and Paul Eyre (Independent Order of Oddfellows Manchester Unity Friendly Society)

Cover picture: Alex Lloyd 2006. The gelding, also called Lloyd sadly died Oct 2012 aged 25

DISCOVERING UPWELL

BIBLIOGRAPHY

Norfolk and Suffolk   W.G. Clarke

The Skaters of the Fens Alan Bloom

The Cycle Magazine from 1925 to 1939 "The boneshaker"
Veteran Cycle Magazine Gerry Moore

The history of the Huddleston family
by Tristram Frederick Croft Huddleston.

History of Norfolk Blomefield

History of Architecture Pro Banister Fletcher

Eau Brink Drainage J G Lenny 1828 1844

Victoria History of Cambridgeshire

Neath Mechanic Institute, City & County of Cardiff

William White's History, Gazetteer, and Directory of Norfolk 1845

Upwell Pharmacy Records from 1895. P Floyd

Reference Section Wisbech Library

Cambridgeshire Libraries

Wisbech and Fenland Museum

Elgoods Brewery Records

Norwich and Norfolk record office

Watson's and Gardner's History of Wisbech

PREAMBLE

After publishing my book called "Outwell in a Nutshell", many people asked me to undertake a similar project for Upwell. I explained to them that the Reverend Richard Jeans had written an excellent little book called "Upwell, History of a Fenland Village" and it is still available. Unfortunately Richard Jeans died before his work was completed, so his daughter, not wanting his valuable work wasted, published his research unfinished in 1987.

Richard Jeans was the rector of Upwell from 1964 to 1972, before taking up a position at Cherry Hinton. During his time at Upwell he became fascinated by our local history and it was his hobby for many years. Following a brief conversation with his wife Pauline, I discovered he would often visit the Norfolk Records office in preference to doing the normal chores around the old vicarage during his few days off. Of course, I am fully aware I could not possible compete with a man of his stature and academic background, as his book clearly illustrates. I am also fully aware of the time it must have taken him to get as far as he did and, if completed, his work would without doubt have been a classic. His excellent research has enabled us a glimpse into our ancient history and we are indebted to him.

The Reverend Richard Jeans with his wife Pauline.

Researching the ancient history of a small village is painstakingly difficult, small sections of information are hidden in the most obscure places. One has to research volumes of material to obtain small amounts of text relating to a particular topic.

As a local history book it is only right we should include a little bit of our ancient history as there are many names and places still around in the village. There is a fine line between what is relevant and interesting and what might be a little tedious and heavy going which is something I am keen to avoid.

The internet is a great starting point for research today, but data found this way has to be treated with great caution. Not all the information found should be regarded as accurate without validation from known reliable root source material. Unfortunately some internet information is at best misleading and all too often quite incorrect. There are endless examples showing obvious errors even to the most inexperienced researcher.

I have encountered many conflicting debates with locals relating to our waterways and other topics over the years but my time spent studying the area's ancient history from the root source has stood me in good stead.

Listening to stories handed down from previous generations can be interesting and sometimes there is a hint of truth in what is said. Seeking reliable information is time consuming and costly and even then mistakes are often made. There are some remarkable recent publications, such as the work carried out during the "Great Fen Project" over the past 30 years that is very useful to the serious researcher. Information obtained from this source is accurate and reliable.

Another reason for being apprehensive about researching the history of Upwell is that there were so many old characters that were well known in Upwell but not to me. I do not have the same "in depth" knowledge relating to modern history as an Upwell native. Being an Outwellian I do not know the little stories surrounding people and places that make interesting reading but I do know one cannot mention Outwell without quickly following with Upwell, in terms of local history, as they were indeed at one time the same place. Even in modern times the two villages are closely connected.

There are many stories in the two Outwell books that reveal some Upwell history. I have on occasions been told by a few Upwellians, they would not buy a book about Outwell which in some ways is a little sad. The two villagers are linked so it is inevitable; Upwell features in the Outwell books and Outwell is frequently mentioned in this book.

Perhaps we should return to the ancient format with a modern twist and call ourselves "Wellin". This might not be as silly as it sounds, having no obvious break between the two villages. The rivers, health centre, farming, the gas works, brass band, the tramway and many other things are a part of both villages.

As I am writing this introduction I can hear the discord being disapprovingly debated. The two villages divorced around the late 12th century and I suppose that is how it will stay.

After much soul searching and many conversations with Upwell folk, I have decided to produce something similar to the first Outwell book, at the risk of being crucified by the many experts out there who possess great knowledge of the village of Upwell. There are ancient tales deeply entrenched into the minds of some that have promoted conflict over the years but I will endeavour to illustrate the facts gained through many years of research. My intention is to produce a book for easy reading, which annoys the academics somewhat, but I see little point in searching my mind and the dictionary for words seldom used just to demonstrate how *"erudite"* I may or may not be.

As already mentioned, Outwell and Upwell have always had a close association historically consequently it is inevitable that research published in the Outwell book will be reiterated but I will endeavour to avoid unnecessary repetition.

It has taken a considerable amount of time to gather and produce an account of Upwell's history; however the vast amount of material obtained will be published in stages, starting with Discovering Upwell.

I have found small mistakes all too often in other work that I have produced and there may be some in this work. Whilst mistakes are never desirable, they are extremely difficult to avoid with this type of book.

Stories that cannot be easily clarified have to be taken at face value but I have to say generally information acquired is sound.

Recording history has to be factual as near as it is reasonably practical, which accounts for the time it has taken to produce this work. I would like to take this opportunity to apologise for any mistakes there may be and sincerely hope that you find some enjoyment reading it.

Thank You
William P Smith
The Lime trees along the north facing wall were planted circa 1860

Upwell village 2005.

THE NORFOLK VILLAGE OF UPWELL

Upwell is a village previously bordering Isle of Ely, and later Cambridgeshire with Norfolk in the diocese of Ely. Upwell was divided by the old Nene but following amalgamation in 1990 it is today solely in the County of Norfolk. Upwell is located approximately 6 miles west of Downham Market and 7 miles south west of Wisbech. It covers approximately 16,700 acres of land and 300 acres of water. The adult population in the year 2000 was in excess of 2240. The population has not grown significantly over the past 100 years as we see the adult population was 2229 in 1911.

The village is supposed to be as "broad as it is long" which might seem contradictory as at one time it was listed as being the longest "parish" in England.

It is known that in medieval times and up to the late 12th century the two villages of Outwell and Upwell together with neighbouring settlements were called Wella or Welle, *(this spelling varied).*

There is strong evidence to suggest the centre of Welle was in the region of Pious Drove *(original spelling)* where a monastic type dwelling existed. Records also suggest Welle was given to the newly formed Abbey of Ramsey *(969 A.D.)* by King Edgar. Before the 13th century "Welle area" consisted of what is now called: Outwell, Upwell, Lakes End, Tips End and Three Holes, parts of Nordelph, Welney and Christchurch *(formally Brymstone Hill).* But of course these modern names did not exist in Saxon days.

Upwell was not mentioned independently in the 11th century when the Domesday Book was completed. There is evidence of names such as Wydestow or wide water (Lakesend, Three Holes area), Walsynham *(around the Outwell aqueduct area),* Shrewsness *(behind Marmont farm)* Brymstone *(Christchurch),* Wellenee *(Welney),* North Dyke *(Nordelph)* and of course Wella or Welle.

There was mention of "Utwell" and "Hupwell" in the 13th century but it is unclear whether this was Outwell or Upwell or in fact both. What is certain, the whole area was called Wella or Welle. How "Welle" was actually pronounced is debateable as the Saxons spoke with emphasis on the last part of some words such as "boata" meaning boat.

Fenland coastline and natural waterways before 13th century

High ground ▒▒▒▒ Wella/e ....Man made cuts after the 12th century- - - -
*The Wellstream from Littleport to Wisbech was the most dominant
waterway in central Fenland dating from before Neolithic times, but
today seems to be a forgotten waterway.*

After the Norman invasion *(1066)* William the Conqueror instructed his trusted followers to collate all England into groups of one hundred settlements and ascertain their value; strangely the area later to become Outwell was of higher value than the future Upwell. A part of Upwell (Welle) was included in the Wisbech hundred other parts were in the Clackclose Hundred. The area was also given sub names such as: Plawfield, Churchfield, Birbeck and Sandilands; these names are still with us today and used by the various drainage boards. In 1202 the Ramsey abbot was granted a charter by King John to hold a market at "Welles". The market was held on Wednesdays and there was a yearly fair on the feast of St. Peter and St. Paul. The Bishop of Ely and the Abbot of Ramsey who were at that time joint lords renewed the charter each year. The market was in existence for about 600 years. In 1864 there seems to have been only a pleasure fair which was held on the 29th and 30th of June. The fair continued well into the 20th century as Mrs Barrowclough the daughter of a doctor, Dr. Burgess, and later a local doctor's wife recalled. She remembers visiting the fair on the banks of the Well Creek opposite St. Peter's church, when she was a child.

By the early 13th century the entire area was taken over by the monks of Ely and Ramsey. In 1291 there were 16 religious houses holding land in the Welle area. The two largest priories were "Mirmound" *(spelling varied)* founded by St. Gilbert *(Gilbertines)* in Upwell and "Molycourt" in Outwell run by the Benedictines *(inventors of Champagne)*. There was also a smaller house, which has been called perhaps mistakenly a priory, called Thirling *(Thurland)*. The Romans visited parts of Upwell and carried out some drainage but the channels cut by the Romans quickly decayed on their exit. The "Pingle" is an ancient word meaning "encircled by water". Much of the area, which was little more than marshland until the monks organised land drainage, was rented out in return for eels as payment. There appear to have been many arguments between the monasteries of Ely and Ramsey as to the amount of eels they should each receive. It was around this period *(13th century)* that the two villages were divided forming Outwell and Upwell. I have seen no conclusive evidence of these two villages being mentioned independently prior to this date.

It was also at this point in time that the name "Welle" was disappearing from documents in favour of names we are familiar with today.

At this time, when Upwell and Outwell became independent, the town status attributed to *Welle* was lost but the town designation lingers on in Upwell.

Later other parishes were being established and laid claim to the area known as North Dyke *(Nordelph)*. Nordelph was divided between 5 parishes: Denver, Upwell, Outwell, Downham Market and Stow Bardolph before becoming independent in the 1930s. Welney and Christchurch became independent following the 1848 Rectories Act. Three Holes, Tips End and Lakesend have remained in the parish of Upwell.

I was once told by a much respected Upwell farmer, events after the 16th century are not real history. We all have thoughts on how history is defined; personally I think as soon as time passes it becomes history. The content of this book deliberately portrays Upwell's history more after the 16th century.

Where possible I have provided evidence to support what I believe is an accurate account of Upwell's history.

Perhaps now is a good time to advise serious students with a desire for more knowledge of Upwell's ancient history to obtain the book written by the Reverend Jeans, it informs us of historical facts and events before 1600 A.D. in great detail. The book may be available from St Peter' Church and local libraries under the international standard book number ....(I.S.B.N). 0 951291106. This is a small hardback costing £10 which should interest the ardent collectors of local history books. There is a copy in the reference section of Wisbech library.

So, if we start our journey through this book with Marmount *(Mirmound or Marmont)* priory we need to know where this Gilbertine Priory was actually sited. I have spoken to many natives of Upwell and have encountered conflicting information. There seems to be some confusion with Thirling Priory as they were indeed near to each other and possibly had close links. Furthermore there is evidence to suggest Thurland *(Thirling)* was not actually a priory at all but a "Grange" or small religious house amongst many in the area. From the following we can see the location of these two historic buildings that were built around the late 12th century.

Thirling is sited as stated by English Heritage. We are not convinced this is correct. There is evidence to suggest it was nearer to the River.

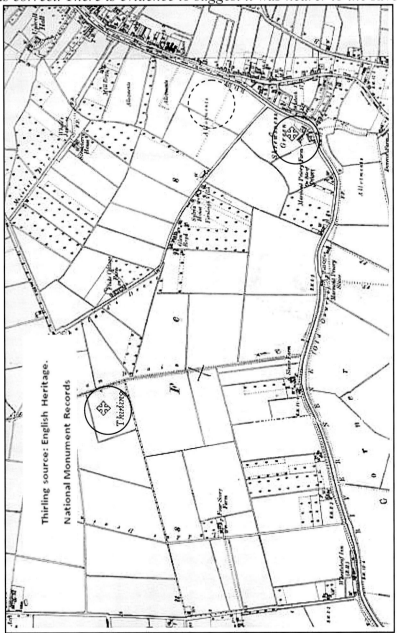

Illustrating the location of Thirling and Marmont Priory.

In February 1188 St. Gilbert, founder of the Houses of Gilbertine the only English monastic order, died at Sempringham, a small isolated village close to what is now the A52 south of Sleaford. He was the son of a Norman knight who came over to England with William the Conqueror.

Among the great number of persons whom he had influenced during his long life was Maud, daughter and heir of Richard de Dunwich and wife of Sir Ralph de Hauvill who held land at Dunton, Doughton and Kettleston in Norfolk. He also owned land in Upwell.

The manor of the Bishops of Ely in Upwell extended into Outwell in Norfolk and adjoined the de Hauvill land which was also on both sides of the river Nene. On the night of the saint's death it is recorded that Maud de Hauvill dreamt that she saw a great company of angels bearing the souls of three of the blessed to heaven, of whom one exceeded the others in glory, and that he was Master Gilbert of Sempringham. It was not, however, until nearly 15 years later that Ralph de Hauvill built on his land in Upwell a small priory for three priests of the Gilbertine Order for the souls of himself and his wife.

The endowment, which was confirmed by King John on 9 May 1204 consisted of all the lands of Ralph and Maud on both sides of the water in Welles, with all their buildings and franchises there, together with the bodies of the founders. The Order was to build a house for their three canons at Ralph's expense, and their only service was to be the payment of 5s. per year as rent, and the reservation of Hauvill's right and that of his heirs to pasture 60 head of cattle with the canon's beasts. The king in confirming the gift stipulated that the canons were to say mass daily in the parish church for the soul of his mother, Eleanor of Aquitaine.

The priory, when handed over to the crown sometime between 1539 and 1553 probably by the Prior - Roger Walker, was at the time inhabited by one Canon and one monk.

Information relating to closure of this priory seems to be contradictory but it is known by 1553 *(Mary I)* it had been abandoned.

Upwell Secondary Modern School children on allotments adjacent to Thurlands (Thirlings) Drove. Circa 1950

Pictured are: Colin Webb, Pat Swann, Ken Frusher, Rodney Rawlings, Michael Vincent, Peter Chapman, David Brooks, Brian Doubleday, Jack Chapman, George Handley, Tony Thorpe, Alan Woolner and Peter Dorling.

Whilst in conversation with his history teacher, Mr Newby, Kenneth Frusher mentioned finding bits of pottery on his father's allotment. The allotments were located adjacent to the Thurlands Drove/March Riverside junction and quite close to the Marmont Priory site.

Mr Newby had told the class, where there are knolls close to old priories and similar buildings, there is a likelihood of there being burial grounds.

The teacher arranged for the boys to have an afternoon "dig" on the allotments. After about an hour they started to uncover human remains which were later identified as being from the 13th century. There were perhaps 10 – 12 skeletons unearthed at this time. The group were instructed by the local authorities to return the bones to the ground, where they remain to this day.

News item reported 1981
A human skeleton found at Marmont Priory Upwell.
The remains consisted of a single adult skeleton from which only part of the hands, both patellae and most of the feet were missing. The bone was in very good condition and most bones were intact, including the skull.

The skeleton is that of an elderly man who was affected by several diseases related to his advanced age, including poor dental health and arthritis. He probably suffered much discomfort towards the end of his life, perhaps suffering from Padgett's disease in his left arm, and with pain in many of his joints, which would have hindered in particular movement of his neck, lower back, fingers, shoulders and hips. He probably had difficulty in chewing and may have been subjected to a largely gruel-based diet.

Although many of the conditions noted above are consistent with the monastic life, it should be noted that they could also indicate a high status lifestyle perhaps with no direct connection to the Priory beyond its use as a final resting place.

Marmont Priory was a Gilbertine priory sited behind the buildings called "Marmont Priory Farm" today. By 1251 the priory held 100 acres of land as a free tenant of the bishop at two shillings per year. The priory was paid £11. 0s. 8d from rents and fisheries from the tenants of Upwell. In 1535 the manor earned £7. 9s. 10d from the Norfolk side and £7. 0s. 1d from the Cambridgeshire side. The site was first granted to Percival Bowes and John Mosyer in 1568. In the 9th year of King James I (1612) the priory was granted to John Eldred and George Whitmore Esq and later it was acquired by Thomas Audley. In the early 19th century Mr. Bacon purchased the site from Mr. Audley. Thomas Audley was a very important landlord in Upwell in the late 18th century and well known friend of Beaupré Bell. His two daughters Ann and Lucy died when quite young and are remembered on a plaque that forms part of the south wall of the St Peter's church (See church section). He later moved to King's Lynn but as another daughter had married an Upwell rector, he maintained links with the village.

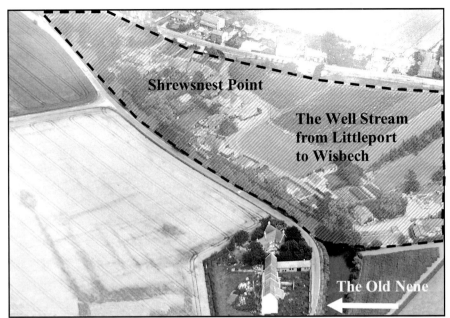

Shrewsnest Point

The Well Stream from Littleport to Wisbech

The Old Nene

S NAVRADY COL

Foundation shadows of Marmont Priory.

At one time before the dissolution, Marmont Priory was indeed a substantial establishment with more than 30 inhabitants.

In February 1536 Thomas Cromwell was instructed to begin the "Dissolution" of the small monasteries in England and Marmont priory was to have been one of them despite being an English order. Thomas Cromwell appeared too lenient so was executed in 1540. The site was granted to Percival Bowes and John Mosyer in 1568 then to John Eldred and George Whitemore Esq in 1612. It seems the buildings remained largely intact until just after the civil war.

For a number of years the remains of the priories belonged to the crown and harsh punishment fell upon those caught taking stone from the ruins. The materials were often used to refurbish and enlarge the new "Churches of England" that previously had been Catholic. St. Clements church Outwell and Upwell's St. Peter's are listed as being essentially 13th century churches but both buildings were greatly enlarged approximately 100 years before the dissolution. I have found no conclusive evidence to suggest these churches benefited from the materials available from the priories.

By the early 18th century, following the "Enclosure Acts" passed by Parliament from 1750 to 1850 which changed the face of Britain's rural landscape, land was being owned and occupied by individuals not directly connected to the monarchy or the church. Building materials were becoming more readily available with the exploitation of the rich turquoise coloured clay found in the previously inundated Fenland.

Brickworks were emerging all over Fenland leaving behind pits that eventually filled with water forming large ponds and small lakes, many of which remain visible today.

A good example of this can be seen with the Vandervell or Colony Lakes adjacent to the Old Bedford River heading towards Manea from Welney.

The colony lake adjacent to the old Bedford River evolved through the extraction of clay that was used to make bricks. The clay was also transported along the Old Bedford River bank by small rail trucks and used to line the river to help prevent leakages in the 1940s.

The priory ruins were becoming a monument to Catholicism, consequently by the late 18th century a blind eye was turned to the pillaging of the priory materials. Local people were not discouraged when removing vast quantities of stone to cover earth floors and improve the structure of their properties.

The remnants of Marmont Priory south-west of Church Bridge

Circa 1855 Tubbs

The thatched cottage far left displaying reclaimed ashlars that were previously part of Marmont priory.

Old ecclesiastical materials could have been recovered during the building of the Rectory now known as Welle Manor Hall but not used on this cottage as it pre-dates the demolition of the previous building on the Rectory site.

There is little doubt in my mind that the materials used to build this cottage were once part of the much grander building called "Mirmont Priory" (Original spelling).

From: Watson, History of Wisbech, 1827. William Watson's description of this cottage mirrors only a small part of the documents seen in the Cambridgeshire archives, saying:

Part of the front range of a medieval building, probably of U-plan, and possibly a lodging or guest house associated with one of the sixteen religious houses established in the Upwell area, now two cottages. Coursed Barnack stone ashlars with only slight disturbance to front wall, some brick repairs to rear wall and partial rebuilding in brick to left hand gable end. Probably cut down when the pan-tiled roof and ridge stacks were built and now of two storeys. On splayed plinth, Ogee headed arch to former central doorway, now blocked, flanked by attached chamfered shafts on octagonal bases with the upper edge splayed. The shafts have been cut down; the one to the north is stepped back at eaves height. Above the doorway is a splayed string-course. Left hand gable end has another original doorway with one side of the jamb chamfered.

William Watson is perhaps the most distinguished local historian there is ever likely to be in this area and it may not be wise to question his superb work but there are a number of indicators that show his account may not be quite right on this occasion. Mr Watson uses terminology such as "possibly and probably," suggesting he was not entirely happy stating his research as fact. The earlier picture of the cottage dated circa 1855 is clearly showing it to be thatched and not pan tiled as mentioned by Watson in 1827.

The 1855 image of the area is most probably that seen by Mr Watson some 28 years before. A Pan tiled roof would not have been replaced by thatch as the reverse practice was normal. Another pointer is the thatch on the cottage appears to look very old. There have been many alterations since the first known picture was taken in comparison to what can be seen today.

Further information from "A History of the County of Cambridge and the Isle of Ely": Wisbech Hundred Outwell and Upwell, Volume 4 where it can be seen:

A house adjoining the school, 180 yards south-west of Upwell church and on the east side of the street, dates from the early 18th century but has been much altered. It is of two storeys with attics. The roof is partly thatched. A stone-walled house on the west side of the street, just north of Lloyds Bank, has a blocked doorway with a four-centred head and semi-octagonal columns with chamfered bases. This feature is probably late 15th-century and may have been reset. Farther south-west on the same side of the street is a three-story house with a late 18th-century front of some merit; the doorway is recessed and has Ionic columns. There are also some diamond-shaped chimney-stacks, which suggest that the building has an earlier date.

Another indicator is, there was a very important religious house located on land that later became the setting for the Upwell Rectory known today as Welle Manor Hall. It would be unlikely another religious establishment would be so close. The colonising monks were very territorial, even towards the hermitages. The materials contained within the cottages are from the 12th-13th century, during that time plans were afoot to build St. Peter's Church casting further doubts on the origin of the building.

On close inspection, the grade II listed cottages contains a mish-mash of materials from the ground level and throughout the building, display only plain and simple stone work. The exterior of these cottages resemble stone walling with the materials picked up at random as seen in Yorkshire or Cornwall rather than a purposely built dwelling. If this building had been purpose built there would have been some very ornate carvings particularly around the windows, the walls would certainly have been uniformed and upright. The foundations and first metre of the stone work that has existed since the property was first constructed is crude and of poor quality. The monks were extremely skilled builders and would not have produced such poor quality workmanship. The only materials found in and around these cottages are flat sided, functionally employed and none with decoration.

The columns each side of the arched door are out of proportion with the setting, they have no purpose and are obviously not original to the present location.

The most significant indicator is the dimensions of this property. Materials contained within this building were the most costly and desirable, usually reserved for high status, substantial buildings resembling cathedrals, large churches and priories. From the earliest known image of circa 1855 these cottages can be seen to be quite modest and not deserving of such high quality materials.

The stories handed down generations seem to fit the suggestion that all the building materials used at this location are reclaimed from a far more substantial building. The ornate carvings that had received skilled work normally associated with these "Barnack Stones" possibly would have been plundered and used in a much more important establishment accounting for their absence.

I believe the building seen on the north flank of the cottages, now a barbers shop, was demolished in the early 1930s and was, of much earlier date perhaps 15th century.

An interesting conversation evolved one day with Mr. Peter Rolfe, an Upwell native. He mentioned he had some carved stones incorporated into his house and many more buried in the garden that may have been part of Marmont Priory. He recalled tales handed down generations that the stones originally came from "Marmont Priory". His house is situated in School Road, which was previously a continuation of Town Street. Marmont Priory was sited on land not more than 300 metres from his house but over the river. I thought it probable that he might be correct with the old tales as historically, when the old priories were plundered the building materials found new homes usually not too far from the source. I asked Peter for a sample of the stone displaying signs of work from a mason so the museum experts could possibly place a date on it. I waited a couple of weeks for the experts from Cambridge to visit and coyly submitted the stone along with my theory.

Much to my delight I received a telephone call from a Mr. Montague, liaison officer from the portable antiquity scheme, in June (2004) confirming our thoughts. Mr. Quinton Carroll, Principal of the Sites and Monuments Records Cambridge, (SMR), examined the stone and informed us that it formed part of a window and was indeed 13th century. The material is Barnack stone of a type typical of that used in the building of priories in the 13th century. Given all the facts, it seems the tales handed down generations are almost certainly true.

These materials from Barnack, south - east of Stamford, were used to build Peterborough and Ely Cathedrals along with many other distinguished buildings. They would have been transported along the medieval Nene. The materials from Barnack were exhausted by AD 1500 having been extensively mined since before Roman times.

It is recorded that the materials used to build Ely Cathedral came along the Nene to Shrewsness Point (near Workhouse Lane Upwell) then along the Well Stream to Ely. This 10th century Benedictine abbey replaced the original 7th century building started by St. Etheldreda, daughter of the king of East Anglia.

Poster trivia: *Confirming the photograph is dated after 1884. Sunlight is a brand of household soap originally produced by the British company Lever Brothers in 1884. It was the world's first packaged, branded laundry soap. It was designed for washing clothes and general household use.*

From the previous photographs it can be seen "more ashlars" (stone blocks) of similar type known to be from the 12th century were used to extend this "grade II listed building" into two storeys some time between 1884 and 1910. It is possible the additional materials were earlier gathered and stockpiled behind the old cottages before finally being used.

I applied the same testing methods to other stones and relics found around the village and discovered much of "Mirmound Priory" most probably still exists. There are no conclusive archive records revealing the actual history of this building and I fully understand my explanation may be considered by some, conjecture.

The most exhilarating realisation rather than a discovery is producing some evidence illustrating the building adjacent to Irene's salon, as it appears today was originally, at least in part, Marmont Priory and not an original purpose built historical dwelling dating from the 13th century.

All the available evidence and the opinion of a few experts on medieval architecture agree this account is probably correct.

Given realistic consideration to the facts, even skeptics must concede there is a strong possibility Upwell holds a little jewel that should be treasured.

The building as seen in 2012 showing the gothic shaped doorway blocked with reused late 12th century ashlar and flanked by stepped multi sided columns.

Cross sectional plan view

The columns each side of the blocked doorway have been described as being hexagonal, semi-hexagonal, or even semi-octagonal. I have called them multi-sided.

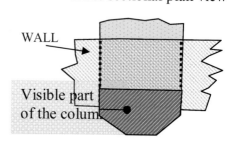

WALL

Visible part of the column

Examples of more surviving 13th century priory

"The beam fragment has guilloche ornament with embattling and is late medieval". It was a wall plate or cornice almost certainly to be from the priory. It is positioned upside down at this location.
Confirmation of the description is by Stephen Haywood FSA, the Norfolk County Council Historical Buildings Officer.

More 13th century historical objects in the same private Upwell garden.

THE ROYAL BRITISH LEGION

The first Upwell and District British Legion hall was erected opposite the entrance gate to the Upwell School playing field in 1946. Mr Hugh Racey of Lode House and Mr. William Hunter made a loan of £300 to enable the branch to purchase two ex-army huts from Matlask in Norfolk. They were erected on land owed by Mr. Racey. The ex-servicemen previously met at the old parish rooms.

In 1947 the "District Branch" had 90 founder members and met up at several locations according to Mr Lionel Barrett. They held a public meeting on 20 January 1947 and agreed to form their own branch in Upwell. In 1949 the branch headquarters was officially formed, the social club was established two years later. The women's section was formed in 1952.

The first British Legion hut with some founder members circa 1948

Standing L/R: Harold Byton, Sidney Gudgeon, Norman Gosbee, Rev. Evans, Ben Braybrook, Neville Boyce, and Frank Russell.
Sitting L/R : Mrs Lockington, Stella Lockington, Hugh Racey, William Hunter, Mrs. Gudgeon, Helen Gosbee, Ron Boyce.

The present site in low side, about 150 metres nearer to Outwell, was purchased in 1962 and Mr. Jeffrey Shepherd was commissioned to construct the new building. Mr George (Jock) Duncan, vice chairman at the time, was given the job of making sure the new building and surrounding gardens were completed on time. The new building was completed at a cost of £2000 and was opened by Mr. Harry Scott MBE. The branch's membership at that time was a healthy 216. George Duncan, a pilot in WWII, was awarded life membership of Upwell and District Royal British Legion in 1964.

In 1977 Mr. Jeffrey Shepherd the club chairman, started a building fund, which enabled alterations and upgrades over the years. Mr Shepherd was a generous benefactor to the Upwell British Legion. There were major alterations in 1983 when the building was extended towards the car park on one side and to the road on the other side. A new roof was installed and the inside was modernised greatly with the corner bar being replaced with a smart new straight bar. There were new carpets, new lighting and furniture. With all the alterations completed there was an official opening on Saturday the 19th November at 8 pm attended by various officials of the Royal British Legion including the Eastern area organiser. The total cost of the refurbishment was around £18,000.

Club membership was originally restricted to ex-servicemen but non-service personnel are now allowed. Membership has been almost as high as 400. The stewardess at this time (1980s) was Kathy Overland who worked closely with Mr. Edward Canham, branch chairman, and Roy Butcher who was the club chairman.

The club is basically a charitable organisation that makes regular contributions to the Earl Haig Poppy Appeal and to the branch benevolent fund, which caters for ex-servicemen and their families who are in need. From the beginning, contributions to the annual poppy appeal has steadily increased and peaked in the late 1990s. Mrs Hazel Medlock was for many years the branch organiser.

In 1981 the branch received a great honour beating over 3,500 branches across the country winning the Haig Cup for being the most efficient

Royal British Legion branch. Mr Barrett confirmed it was the first National recognition the branch had received since its formation.
Previously the Upwell branch had been voted the best branch in Norfolk six times from 1981 to 1997.

The Upwell and District Royal British Legion dinner March 1976

Mr. George (Jock) Duncan, vice chairman of the branch, Major John Rivers, Mr Walter Reedman, branch chairman, Mr. Harry Payne, branch president, Mr Lionel Barrett, branch secretary and treasurer, Lilian Heanes, president of the women's section, Mrs. Ruby Allen, chairman of the women's section. Mrs. I. Barrett, secretary of the women's section, Mrs Thelma Butcher, vice chairman of the women's section.

Illustrating the certificates and souvenir cups awarded to the Upwell and District Branch in recognition and appreciation of being the most efficient and progressive branch in Norfolk 30 September 1975.

An important day in the "clubs" diary is the annual tribute to those who had died during military conflicts. The parade on 13th November 1983 is worth recording as it was typical of the "clubs" activities during Armistice Sunday.

The Peterborough Highland Pipe Band led the parade at both Upwell and Outwell. At Upwell's war memorial, flags were carried by Mrs. Thelma Butcher on behalf of the British Legion Women's section and Mr. Norman Hines, on behalf of the Legion's men's section.

T. Butcher col

Thelma Butcher and Edward Canham with the Standard of the British Legion at St. Peter's church Upwell on this occasion.

The Rev Ray Wallis and the Rev David Nash conducted a service and Nicky Allan was the organist. Christopher Swann and Mr. Stephen Middleditch sounded the Last Post and Reveille. A roll of honour was led by Mr. Albert Feary, chairman of Upwell (Norfolk) British Legion, and Mr John Bays read Binyons Lines to the Fallen. Wreaths were laid by Mr Roy Butcher on behalf of the Legions men's section, Mrs Lillian Barrett on behalf of the women's section. Mrs Jill Gooch laid a wreath on behalf of Upwell (Isle) Parish Council. The parade then assembled in the Methodist Chapel where the Rev Nash preached a sermon. Mr. Dewdney read the lesson. About 100 people attended the service and the organist was Miss. Nora Fielder.

At Outwell in the afternoon, the parade assembled at Beaupré School under the guidance of parade marshal Sergeant Major Instructor Ivor Longmuir of Outwell. In the parade were members of Upwell St. Peter's church choir, members of the village branch of the British Legion: The "Legion's" Women's section, The Outwell Army cadets, Outwell Fire Service and some Outwell Parish Councillors. At St. Clements Church, Rev Ray Wallis conducted a service and Rev Ray Clues O.B.E gave the sermon. Mr. George Bucklow read the roll of honour and Mr. Stanley Booly read the lesson. Organist was Mr. Stanley Simmons. After the service they moved outside to the War Memorial where Mr. Louis Doubleday gave the tribute. Wreaths were laid by Mr. George (Jock) Duncan on behalf of the British Legion, Mrs. Mary Carter on behalf of the Legions women's section, Captain Austin Ward on behalf of the Army Cadets, Sub officer Robin Ward for the fire service, Mr. Neville Laws for Norfolk Parish Council, and Mrs. Iris Risebrow on behalf of Isle Parish Council. Mr. Swann and Mr. Middleditch played the last post. After the two minutes silence the parade marched back to Beaupré School to the sounds of the Peterborough Highland Pipe Band. The day of remembrance is attended by few these days but those who gave their lives will never be forgotten and are recorded elsewhere in this book.

One young man who originally came from Sevenoaks in Kent narrowly missed death whilst serving with the Royal Irish Rifles in the First World War. He was the steward at Upwell British Legion club for many years. Mr. Horace Henry (George) Bennett was seriously injured in his leg by shrapnel. His injury did not heal so he was admitted to

Roehamstead Hospital London to have the leg amputated below the knee.

During the Second World War he was a member of the Observer Corps using an observation post near Green Lane Upwell. He moved to Church Drove Outwell in 1949 and commenced employment with the British Legion; he was the steward until his retirement in 1964. This was a job he loved and was very much respected by the club members. He was familiar with most village folk who would marvel at that way he rode his cycle coping with his disability extremely well.

Bar Steward: Mr Horace George Bennett 1899- 1985

Mr Bennett is seen serving members:
Jack Swann, Lionel Barnett and Ben Braybrook in the original British Legion building in 1955.

Lionel Barrett circa 1955

Thelma Butcher col

Thelma Butcher col

Mrs. Welch, Ollie Shepherd at the piano, Mrs. Skeels, Thelma Butcher, Mrs. Brooks, Dolly Hensby.

The premises had a major overhaul in 2005. The open day to mark the £10k refurbishment was held Saturday 29th January with a new dance floor, new tables and chairs, curtains, alterations to the bar and the building was redecorated throughout. The club had over 250 members at this time that relied greatly on Alison Saunders, Teresa Evans and Jenny Morton to keep the new bar shipshape.

Mr & Mrs Roger Mungham, Barry Evans & Mick Winters.

Photograph exhibition Saturday 29th January 2005.

BRANCH OFFICERS OF THE UPWELL ROYAL BRITISH LEGION
From 1946

Date	Branch President
46-47	Dr. J. Barrowclough
47-52	Archdeacon S. Evans
52-72	C Clark
72-94	H Payne
94-01	L Barrett
01-	G Duncan

Date	Branch Chairman
46-47	H Payne
47-50	C Clark
50-53	S Booley
53-78	W Reedman
78-99	E Canham
99-08	R Houghton
08-2012	D Gray

Date	Branch Treasurer
46-48	H Racy
48-49	S Guddin
49-50	G Barry
50-83	L Barrett
83-87	J Ridway
87-89	L Barrett
89-99	P Doran
99-03	J Lee-Manning
	R Clark
	M Winters
	S Jennings
2012	P Gray

Date	Branch Secretary
46-47	H A Jones
47-50	F W Russell
50-60	L C Doubleday
60-62	Rev S Jones
62-91	L Barrett
91-99	G R Acton
99-2012	M D Winters

Branch Vice Chairmen from 1947 include:
C Clark, B V Braybrook, S Cragg, S Booley and G M (Jock) Duncan.

Poppy organisers included: Lilly Barrett, Elsie Morton, Hazel Medlock, Michael & Susan Winters, Pauline Gray, Pat Parsons, Peter Morgan and Sally Almer along with many volunteer collectors since 1952.

CLUB OFFICIALS OF THE UPWELL ROYAL BRITISH LEGION
From 1946

Date	Club President
46-52	C Clark
52-67	H Racy
67-78	J Shepherd
78-04	G Duncan
04-	Mrs T Butcher
	D Overland
	M Ellis

Date	Club Chairman
46-63	W Reedman
63-78	G Duncan
78-82	J Shepherd
82-90	R Butcher
90-93	J Bays
93-99	E Canham
99-2000	H Allen
00-2001	R Acton
01-03	P Boddle
03-04	B Snellgrove

Date	Club Secretary
46-56	V Barrett
56-63	L Doubleday
63-78	S Booley
78-84	G Bucklow
84-99	H Allen
99-2003	Mrs P Thulborn
04-2012	M Winters

Date	Club Treasurer
46-58	R Tunnard
58-68	J Fennessy
68-84	J Bays
84-87	M Pope
87-00	P Doran
00-03	B Snellgrove
03	P Broddle

Club Vice Chairmen included: G Duncan, W Reedman, R Butcher, H Allen, G Bucklow, J Bays, E Canham, J Wilson, R Houghton, P Boddle, D Overland and P Morton.

WOMEN SECTION OF THE UPWELL ROYAL BRITISH LEGION
From 1952

Date	Women's President
52-78	Mrs L Heanes
78-80	Mrs A Carter
80-95	Mrs L Heanes
95-	Mrs L Barrett

Date	Women's Chair
52-55	Mrs V West
55-60	Mrs E Morton
60-62	Mrs M Carter
62-65	Mrs E Morton
65-77	Mrs M Smith
77-99	Mrs R Allen
99-	Mrs T Butcher

Date	Women's Secretary
52-54	Mrs D Foster
54-56	Mrs M Carter
56-92	Mrs L Barrett
92-95	Mrs D Roper
95-2000	Mrs L Allen
00-12	Mrs S Elmer

Date	Vice Chairperson
52-59	Mrs E Morton
59-65	Mrs M Smith
65-77	Mrs R Allen
77-99	Mrs T Butcher
99-2000	Mrs R Allen
00-	Mrs B Corney

Date	Treasurer
52-54	Mrs M Braybrook
54-67	Mrs M Jones
67-72	Mrs P Hunt
72-74	Mrs M Evens
74-96	Mrs D Hines
96-20 12	Mrs P Gray

Stewards and stalwarts:
G Bennett, Roy &Thelma Butcher, Phil Myers, Jack & Phil Bassett, June Chapman, Ken Allday, Harry Bell, Kath & Don Overland, Bob Bowie, Mick Ellis, John Pope & Maureen Cobb.

Mick & Sue Winters, David & Pauline Gray keep the fires burning in 2012.

PUBLIC HOUSES

There have been many inns, pubs and ale houses in Upwell over the years, providing a service that is in steep decline today. In the days before computers and television, the village pub was one of the few places outside the church for social gatherings. The local pub was a focal point after a hard day's work for many but was often the cause of much hardship. There are endless tales of men spending their money in the pub whilst their families go hungry. The local pub in general, was an important part of the community and often did far more good than harm.

There were spin-off activities organised by pub licensees for the families of the patrons such as bus trips, days out at the races and national events. Most of these activities evolved after the Second World War. The pub landlords and patrons would organise trips to see special events like boxing matches, the speedway and football finals. The boot of the coach would be loaded with beer and treats of course! There were the darts, crib and sometimes bowls matches taking place within the pub curtilage. Many pubs organised special treats for the children like trips to the seaside and Christmas parties. These events were eagerly anticipated each year and provided a close community spirit. The motivation behind running a regional village pub today seems to have moved away from social integration.

How things have changed with the big screen in the pubs receiving live coverage of international events and the patrons silently glued to their seats occasionally jumping up to express their views before settling back down to another bout of enthusiastic viewing.

There were more than twenty public houses in Upwell, sixteen can be listed with some degree of assurance. If one considers the old communities in the area of Welle there were over sixty such establishments, many of which are listed on the internet.

There exists an interesting growing website by Richard Bristow of Dereham called "Norfolk Pubs", it is well worth a browse.

In this book we will attempt to record most of the public houses in Upwell but of course, there may be someone who will tell us about the ones we have missed.

34

Locations identified by: **O**rdnance **S**urvey National **G**rid **R**eference

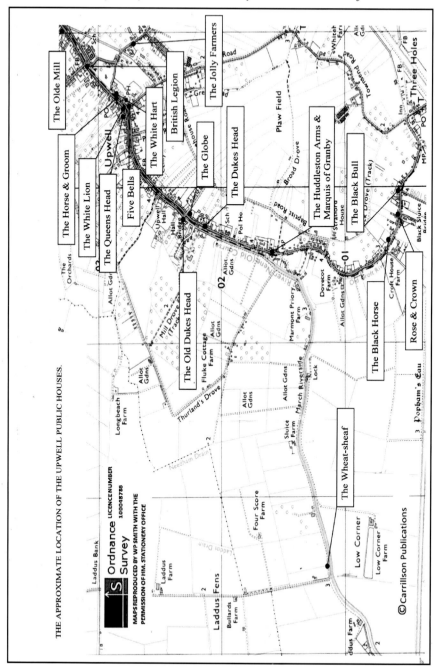

THE APPROXIMATE LOCATION OF THE UPWELL PUBLIC HOUSES.

Ordnance Survey
LICENCE NUMBER
100048785

MAPS REPRODUCED BY W P SMITH WITH THE
PERMISSION OF HM. STATIONERY OFFICE

©Carrillson Publications

The Olde Mill

The Jolly Farmers

British Legion

The White Hart

The Globe

The Dukes Head

The Huddleston Arms &
Marquis of Granby

The Black Bull

Three Holes

The Horse & Groom

The White Lion

The Queens Head

Five Bells

The Old Dukes Head

The Black Horse

Rose & Crown

The Wheat-sheaf

The public houses listed are essentially those found in Upwell and not the surrounding villages.

The Black Bull. Bull Bridge. OS NGR TF 4998 0055 *Brewery:* Elgoods. A collection of papers held by the Rev. James Porter (Baptist minister) in the mid 19th century suggests the Black Bull and associated buildings have existed from 1662 but most likely as a pub only since 1830.

This collection of deeds relates to property containing a pub, barber's shop and smithy. It was held firstly by the Baker family for over a hundred years, before subsequently passing to the Wooll family for a short period. According to a conveyance listed in an old existing calendar of the collection, the property was then sold to the Rev. James Porter. The deeds, consisting mainly of mortgages, date from 1662 to 1841.

The deeds show the properties came into the possession of George Wooll, a wealthy land owner and farmer, of Upwell in the Isle of Ely, Cambridgeshire circa 1830. The Rev Porter's documents are very detailed showing ownership of adjacent buildings e.g.

Lease for a term of 4 1/5 years, annual rent £8 dated 27 Apr 1831; i) George Wooll of Upwell, Cambridgeshire, farmer and grazier; ii) Thomas Baker of Upwell, Norfolk, blacksmith; One blacksmith shop with shoeing shed at Upwell, Norfolk opposite a public house called the Black Bull and now in the tenure of Thomas Baker.

*The bridge over the Old Welney River and the public house no longer
exist but the area is known to this day as Bull Bridge.*
The Black Bull appears to have been separated from adjacent buildings
and sold to Elgoods of Wisbech by George Wooll of The Hall
Christchurch circa 1830. Hugh Wooll's daughter Anne married into the
West family who are still living in the Upwell area today. The Wooll
family was amongst the area's elite in the mid 19th century. In 1910
Walter Wooll West, of Needham Hall, Elm, was High Sheriff of
Cambridgeshire. Hugh Wooll West, of Croft house Upwell, was also on
the High Sheriff's nomination roll in 1916.

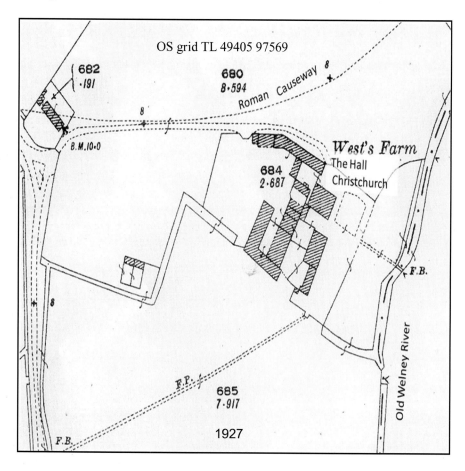

Wooll's farm at Christchurch, later to become West's farm was sited in a prime historic trading location. There may have been habitation at the site for centuries being so close to the two most ancient features in this part of Fenland. There are many farms still located close to the Roman causeway stretching from Peterborough to Denver that can be used to accurately plot the course of the causeway.

Black Bull licensees:
Thomas Clarke 1830, Thomas Baker 1836, James May 1839, Edward Bellamy 1845, Henry Bellamy 1846, John Ogden 1850, George Swann 1854, John Giddens 1858, John Bird 1864, William Felstead 1877, William Overland 1890, Richard Pratt 1904, Walter Stevenson 1909, John Turner 1925 and Evangelina Turner 1935. Evangelina left the Dun Cow Christchurch to take over the Bull. George Amps 1936 was the last keeper when the pub closed in 1965.

Bull Bridge

The Black Bull Bridge gave passage over a redundant waterway with many names that included: the Wellstream, the Ouse, the old Welenee River and the Croft.

The Black Horse. Croft Road (Town Street) OS NGR TF 4970 0061.
Breweries: Frank Mills, Hall, Cutlack & Harlock, Steward and Patteson.
The Black Horse public house was located at Croft Road, formerly Town Street. It was originally supplied by Mills' brewery of Wisbech and owned by George William Mills and later Frank Mills brewer and maltster. There is little sign of the Black Horse today, it was demolished circa 2000. The last remnants of the south wall, displaying a few Queen Ann style bricks, were demolished June 2012.

Remnants of the Black Horse

Mills Brewery Wisbech, located on the site now occupied by the police station. Picture taken from the Institute tower, possible by Lilian Ream.

Note the railway trucks from the Harecroft Road station. The track passed by Barclays bank and terminated close to the old Wisbech Bridge.

Black Horse Licensees:

William Doyle 1830, James Markilee 1845, Jacob Markilee 1851, Sarah Markilee 1864, Thomas Brabrook 1868, William Ladds 1879, Jewson Ward 1881, Thomas Arbin 1883, Samuel Rowell 1892, John Ward 1896, Robert Bradshaw 1900, William Wiles 1912, Robert Hardy 1922, Bernard Warby 1932, Arthur Kitchen 1935, Ellen Kitchen 1944, Whartley Green 1947, Walter Casbin was the keeper when the pub closed in 1965.

The Black
Horse
circa 1912

Old Dukes Head. New Bridge. OS. NGR TF 4981 0230. *Breweries:*
Hall of Upwell, Cutlack & Harlock (Ely Ales), Steward & Patteson.

Circa 1920

Circa 1880

C Chapman

Old Dukes Head licensees: Nathaniel Booth 1830, John Hawkin 1845, James Ryan 1850, John Hill 1854, John Walker 1864, Henry Clarke 1869, George Thacker 1877, Joseph Lawrence 1879, James Overland 1896 to circa 1910, Charles Bensley 1911, Mrs Harriett Bensley 1929, Jack Nutt up to 1939, Albert G Melton 1939, Joseph Farrow 1960 was the keeper when the pub closed in 1962.

G Melton

Pictured are Mrs Lily Melton, Frank (Dick) Melton and Albert Melton. Albert G Melton was the Old Dukes Head landlord from 1939 to 1960.

In the early 1950s a local doctor from a nearby practice thought he could not be seen having a pint in the same place as his patients so he sat alone in the Old Dukes Head cellar. How things have changed since those days, one certainly might enjoy the company of the local GP in a bar today but I suspect the ones I know would not treat you to a pint!

Dukes Head. (The Iron Duke). School Road, formerly Town Street. OS. NGR TF 4975 0209. *Breweries:* (Ely Ales) Cutlack & Harlock, Bullards.

Commissioned by E. Loughlin

Licensees:
Edward Edwards 1830, James Andrews 1836, John Sherwing 1839, John Baker 1845, Edward Baker 1875, Joseph Lawrence 1881, John Maywood 1883, Frederick Ward 1888, Charles Bensley 1901, Walter Stevenson 1908. The last keeper appears to have been Clement Deptford, the public house closed circa 1930.

The Dukes Head 2012

Marquis of Granby & Huddleston Arms. School Road.
OS. NGR TF 4958 0154 *Breweries:* Gray & Hart (Upwell) Frank Mills,
Hall, (Ely Ales) Cutlack & Harlock, Steward & Patteson.

John Manners was the eldest son of the 3rd Duke of Rutland. He died
before his father and therefore gained his father's secondary title "The
Marquis of Granby". The "Manners" had ancestral connections with
Upwell, Outwell and surrounding area.
John Manners was once described by King George II as "a sot, a bully
and a drunken brawler. Having said that, King George himself appears
not to have enjoyed the respect of the populace, as it was said he was
arrogant, pompous and boring.

Manners enjoyed horse racing, drinking and gambling and was
generally regarded as a most unlikely hero. But in later life he certainly
turned out to be just that. Following a stint as MP for Grantham and
Cambridgeshire, John Manners was made a Colonel in the Royal Horse
Guards in 1758 and later promoted to Lieutenant-General. He gained
much respect for his acts of bravery, not only from his superiors but
also his men during several battles including the Battle of Minden
where the French were defeated in 1759.

The Marquis lead from the front, probably well inebriated, which
gained the admiration of his men. He had a reputation for looking after
his men and was idolised for his common touch.

When the Marquis of Granby died in 1770 there was a genuine sense of
grief across the nation. Many of his soldiers had taken to being
publicans and named their pubs after him. It is likely the Marquis of
Granby public house in Upwell was opened between 1770 and 1800. I
have been able to pinpoint most Upwell pubs very accurately using a 10
figure ordnance survey grid number but could not find the location of
the Marquis of Granby public house. I spoke to many old Upwell locals

and people who have researched Upwell pubs in the past but could not locate where it was sited.

During the research of the "Huddleston Arms" I noticed the last recorded licensee of the Marquis of Granby was a Daniel Lock 1850. It is unlikely the pub closed during this period as public houses were becoming very popular.

The Huddleston arms appeared on the scene in the early 1850s and the first licensee was Daniel Lock. It seemed plausible the Marquis of Granby had a name change to the Huddleston Arms.

We carried out a meticulous survey of what remains of the Huddleston Arms and discovered the building dates from at least the early 18th century further enhancing our theory.

The remains of the Huddleston Arms adjacent to the road, it was for many years called Town Street.

Showing the remains of the Huddleston Arms along the south flank
The final clue can be seen in the 1848 Upwell tithe map where it shows
the Marquis of Granby public house to be located where the remains of
the Huddleston Arms is today.
The following statement appeared in a London newspaper.

THE LONDON GAZETTE, DECEMBER 8, 1863.
To be sold, pursuant to an Order of the High Court of Chancery, made
in a cause of Gray v. Austin, with the approbation of the Master of the
Rolls, in two lots, by Mr. William Elworthy, the person appointed by the
said Judge, at the Huddleston Arms Inn, Upwell, in the county of
Cambridge, on Wednesday, the 23rd day of December, 1863, at six
o'clock in the evening precisely.
All that freehold dwelling-house, homestall, and premises, with 15a. 0p.
23r.- (more or less), of land lying under the same, partly grass, and
partly arable, now in the occupation of Mr. Samuel Waters, being Lot 1.

*And all that freehold piece of land called the Half Acres, containing
14a. 0p. 25r. (more or less), between lands of the Rev. G. J. Huddleston,
and the Corporation of the Sons of the Clergy, now in hand, being Lot 2.
Particulars whereof may be had, gratis, of Messrs. Metcalfe, Solicitors,
Wisbeach; Messrs. Hensman and Nicholson, Solicitors, No. 25,
College-hill, London ; St. Pierre Butler Hook, Esquire, Solicitor, No. 9,
Lincoln's-inn-fields, London; William Ludlam Ollard, Esquire, Solicitor,
Upwell; and of the Auctioneer, Upwell.*

The above clearly illustrates the Huddleston Arms existed in 1863 and
it was sited between land belonging to The Rev George James
Huddleston. Both Peter Huddleston and the Rev G J Huddleston had
estates in Upwell around the mid 19th century.
So where did the name Huddleston come from and why change the
name of this old public house?
The Reverend George James Croft was born in 1802 in Winchester but
along with his brothers and father took the name Huddleston in 1819,
George Huddleston was godfather to George Croft's father.
His father was residuary legatee for George Huddleston. In this case:
*The person or persons named in a will to receive any residue left in an
estate after the bequests of specific items are made provided he took the
arms and name of Huddleston.*
This gave them the right to the Huddleston coat of arms bringing with it
some privileges and status.
The Rev Huddleston came to Upwell circa 1828 to live with and assist
the Rev William Gale Townley. He fell in love with William Lee's
daughter; William Lee was one of Upwell's most prominent land
owners at the time and he lived at Lee House, Town Street. Ann Lee,
born 1803, and George James Huddleston married in Upwell St Peter's
church 1832. This seemed to set a trend within the two families as
George's brother Peter married Ann's sister Elizabeth and another
brother, Purefoy, married the daughter of the eldest sister, Mary.
It appears William Lee did not have a surviving son so managing the
estate fell to his daughters and of course their husbands. Given the size
of William Lee's estate, the Huddleston family became very important
in Upwell. The Rev George Huddleston had Upwell Hall built for him

and he was the first occupier. The Rev Huddleston was known to be a benevolent man and continued William Lee's work in helping the poor. This may have been why the Marquis of Granby pub became named the Huddleston Arms Inn in honour of the Rev George James Huddleston.

The Rev George J Huddleston

At the rear of the Huddleston Arms with friends of Valerie Cooper and Pam Myers, children of the Huddleston Arms last licensees.

Licensees:
(Marquis of Granby) *It is believed this public house existed many years before 1830.* James Cassidy Nugent 1830, William Means 1836, William Rogers 1845, Daniel Lock 1850. It appears Daniel Lock was the tenant when the premises had the name change.
(Huddleston Arms)
Daniel Lock 1854, William Fisher 1875, Edward Hillard 1882, Lupton Pell 1883, William Green 1888, George W Spurling 1890, John T Hunt 1892, William Hardy 1896, Fredrick Rolfe 1912, Harriet Rolfe 1922, Josiah Parker 1928, Bernard Richardson 1829, Jack Swann 1949, Lesley Myers, the pub closed in 1963.

49

Pictured are Les and Phyl Myers, the last licensees of possibly the oldest public house in Upwell dating from the 18th century.

Huddleston Arms

Huddleston Coat of arms

The Rose and Crown. OS NGR 49712 00595. Croft Road, (Town Street) *Breweries:* Hogg & Sebbings (Setchy) Bullards.
Licensees: John Berry 1800, John Berry Jr 1819, James Turner 1830, George Charlton 1846, Henry Burrell 1865, John Deptford 1875, William Deptford 1877, John Deptford second term 1877 to 1888, Charles Overland 1890, Henry Warby 1905, George Overland 1912 to 1948, Cyril Judd from 1948 to 1968, M Sooley? when the pub closed.

A modern picture of the Rose and Crown circa 2006

Many years ago whilst researching the activities of Dr Tubbs, I came across a sad story in the Wisbech Advertiser. Unfortunately I have been unable to find my notes written at the time but I can still remember some of the details. In 1851 there was a tragic accident outside the Rose and Crown public house.

The paper reported a Mr (sic) Cook falling from his "Gill" and the wheels severed both his legs. He was carried into the Rose and Crown and Dr Tubbs was called. Unfortunately Dr Tubbs was unable to save the man's life.

We are of the opinion a "Gill" in this case was a special two piece horse drawn lorry used to transport large tree trunks.

Tubbs/Chapman circa 1860

C Chapman circa 1880

The Globe Inn. OS NGR TF 49726 02310 School Road.
Breweries: Elgoods.
Originally the Globe was a small beer house operating under the shadow of the Old Dukes Head opposite and the nearby Dukes Head. The building was enlarged circa 1864 soon after Elgoods took possession.
A stranger to the pub struck up a conversation with a well known local one night. "They'll never solve it, never," says Mally, the local coalman, sitting with a bottle of brown ale in the corner of the pub. "How can they? They've got no evidence."
Mally Pope is a long time regular of the pub and a well known local character, who lives in a house called the "Vatican" opposite the pub.
Mally was drawn into a conversation about the brutal double murders of a spinster dog-breeder and her ageing mother which shocked the community. The women were repeatedly stabbed, and left to die on the floor of their front room at their home located in a drove past the Pingle Bridge.
Mally had no idea who he was talking to at the time and was shocked to see his comments appear in the Independent newspaper written by John Davidson on Saturday 23 January 1999.
The perpetrator of the crime was in fact caught and subsequently jailed for life.
Kevin Cotterell, 33, of Pentney, Norfolk, pleaded guilty to stabbing to death 45-year-old Janice Sheridan and Connie Sheridan, 79, at their home at the Pingle, Upwell, Norfolk, in January 1999.

Janice aged 45 and her mother Connie Sheridan aged 79.
They will always be remembered.
There is no known relationship between the two women and a former landlord of the pub whose son was tragically killed.

Acknowledgment: Elgoods Brewery North Brink Wisbech.

We are indebted to Elgoods for the following list of tenants, with the exception of the first three entries that may not have been employed by the brewery.

LIST OF TENANTS

DATE	TENANT	START DATE	END DATE
1863	GEORGE HILL	1863	N/K
1871	GEORGE W THACKER	G Thacker moved to the Old Dukes head whilst his wife looked after the Globe	
1875	SUSANNA THACKER		
1877	JOSEPH LAWRENCE		
1879	R T WRIGHT		
1880	EDWARD FRYETT		
1880	WILLIAM HINKINS		
1881	JOHN JUDD		
1891	JOSEPH LAWRENCE		
1924	JOHN ROBERT FRANCIS		
1954	JACK OSWALD WINTERS	04/08/1954	07/12/1973
1973	G A C SHERIDAN	07/12/1973	16/09/1976
1976	K M HIRCOCK	16/09/1976	08/04/1981
1981	RH BOWIE	08/04/1981	21/01/1988
1988	DB MORGAN	21/01/1988	18/01/1990
1990	E G MIERAU	18/01/1990	19/05/1993
1993	MRS N MASTERS	19/05/1993	05/10/1994
1994	C DURKIN	05/10/1994	31/05/1995
1995	K THOMPSON	31/05/1995	04/11/1996
1996	MRS S A BRADDICK	04/11/1996	11/07/1997
1997	MRS J A ASPLIN	11/07/1997	21/05/1998
1998	DUNCAN LAWTON	21/05/1998	
2006	LESLEY LAWTON	01/09/2006	

George Thacker and Joseph Lawrence left the Globe to move to the Old Dukes Head, Joseph Lawrence moved back to the Globe in 1891.

In 1877 the annual pub rent was £10, ordinary farm labourers were getting around ten shillings (50p) a week at that time and beer was around 2d a pint. Roughly equivalent to half of one new pence.

In 2003, whilst employed by Nestlé Purina, I had reason to work with some Dutch contractors. I arranged accommodation for the company owner at the Crown Hotel Outwell. He was intensely interested in our local history and particularly the 17th century drainage undertakings. I spent a couple of evenings at the Crown with him making comparisons with the drainage issues affecting Holland and the Fens. During the course of our conversations the name Upwell cropped up quite a bit and so he was familiar with the village name.

About three months after he had returned to Holland I received the photograph below. It was sent to me by the Dutch contractor, who was on holiday in South Africa and came across this grave purely by chance.

From the church records.
Baptised, June 8 1862 Lawrence Edward son of Joseph & Sarah otp (of this parish) labourer.

It is by no means certain why Edward Lawrence found himself in South Africa.

There are a few possibilities including staying there to hunt for gold after the 2nd Boer War.

If that is the case then he must have been successful judging by the expensive headstone on his grave at Pilgrims Rest.

His brother, Joseph Lawrence, was the licensee of the Globe and Old Dukes Head public houses around the time Edward died.

The Queen's Head OS NGR TF 5048 0278. Town Street.
Breweries: Frank Mills. Cutlack & Harlock
Licensees: Simon Melton 1830, Francis Smith 1836, William Hopkins 1851, Wallman Hucknell 1868, James Frusher 1877, Elizabeth Smith 1880, Mary Ann Rallison 1892, John Pitts 1904, James W Scott 1916, Alex King 1929, Percy Johnson 1936. Percy's wife, Louise ran the pub until the pub closed circa 1958.

The Queens Head and Wallman Hucknell are listed in the 1869 Post Office Directory.

The Queen's Head early 1950s

This photograph is thought to have been taken by Dr William Tubbs Pre-1870. The gentleman seated is Charles Chapman.

The picture is dated around 1868, the licensee at this time was Wallman Hucknell. The Queen's Head was adjacent to a building that was once a school and later the workshop for Tommy Hinds the stone mason, Harold Means and most recently Colin Chamberlain.

White Lion OS NGR TF 5053 0281 Town Street, grade II listed.
Breweries: Hogge & Sebbings Ltd, Bullard, Watney.
This public house was originally owed by Dennis and Charles Herbert & Co. They operated from Setch Bridge Brewery before joining up with William and George Hogge. The partnership later included Charles Sebbings.
Licensees: Luke Bowell 1805, Sarah Chamberlain 1830, Benjamin Notson 1836, William Brown 1865-90, Walter Horn 1916, Bert Overland 1928, Harry Crane 1962, Melvyn Dewsbury 1971, Nigel Carter was the last licensee as the pub closed in 1985.

In around 1920, a son of the White Lion landlord, Cyril Horn, stood on a box to serve the customers. He was a small lad and could not reach the pumps without standing on a box.
One night a customer said to him, "Will you pull me a pint baby boy"? This coined the phrase "baby Horn". It was an affectionate nickname that stayed with Babs Horn all his life.
Babs, and his brother, Dennis, became nationally famous for ice skating and cycling. More about the Horn family elsewhere in the book.

Harry Crane Licensee in the 1960s
Whilst undertaking improvements to the pub in the 1960s, workmen found some interesting relics hidden inside a wall. They came across a quantity of old clay pipes in near perfect condition. Clay pipes were commonly used from the 16th century right through to the 1940s.

58

Horse and Groom OS NGR TF 5057 0286.
Brewers: Hogg, Herbert & Hogg, Hogg & Sebbings.
Licensees: John Lowe 1830, William Cragg 1836, George Jermey 1864,
George Jarmany 1865, Mrs Ann Jarmany 1877, Robert Johnson 1890,
Arthur Calver 1900. The pub closed circa 1930.

The Horse & Groom Town Street

A few years ago I was given this interesting recollection by a
relative of Arthur Calver, Arthur Calver was the landlord of
the Horse and Groom pub around 1900.

*My name is Alfred Calver, I have been asked to put on record
what Upwell was like in the early 1900s. I was born 1911 at
the Horse and Groom pub, which is two houses down from the
Post Office. There were twelve other pubs in Upwell, namely,
The Queens Head and The Five Bells at Church Bridge, The*

Globe and The Old Duke's Head at Hall Bridge, The Duke's Head and The Huddleston Arms at School Road, The Black Horse at Dovecote Road, The Rose and Crown at Croft Road, The Bull at Bull's Bridge, The Jolly Farmers at Small Lode and The Wheat-sheaf at March Riverside. Now only the Globe remains. (This was written in the late 1970s. The Five Bells was re-opened later).

When I was young there were only a few motor cars in Upwell. These were owned by Doctors and a few of the better off. The windmill in those days was in working order and farmers used to take corn to be ground there. There was no bus service then and people such as fruit growers and farmers would travel to Wisbech by horse and cart. We had a tram service which ran to Wisbech about three times a day for sixpence return, 2p in new money.
The Upwell tram station was a very busy place, as nearly all produce from the district was carted by tram. In the fruit season I have seen long queues from Church Bridge one way to Lister's Road the other, with a policeman on traffic duty. We also had barges which carted bricks and coal. These barges were of the old wooden type and were drawn by a horse on a long rope and the lighter-man used to steer with a long pole. The last barges to be seen on the river, just before the last war, were made of steel and carted sugar beet. These were pulled by boats.

Main roads were made of gravel stones which were steam "rollered" in, but all by-roads were ground in by the iron rim wheels of carts and wagons, this would make large ruts in the road.
There were three blacksmiths in the village, there are none today. Their work was chiefly shoeing horses. There was Mr Butler at Hall Bridge, Mr Walter Horn behind the White Lion pub and Mr. George Sraithee (Smithee) in front of the Horse

and Groom pub. During the First World War they were all making horseshoes for the army.

At Church Bridge every year we used to have a fair, with all kinds of stalls. These would be both sides of the river and would cause all kinds of hazards, even in those days.

On farms there were no tractors and all work was done by horses. Boys and girls left school at fourteen years of age. The boys went to work on the land and the girls went into domestic service as there was no other work available. In those days you had to behave yourself. Punishment was two strokes of the cane on each hand. It was also expected of you to touch your cap to your headmaster and other dignified persons of the village.

Jolly Farmers. *(The Ragged Louse)* OS NGR TF 5096 0265 Small Lode

Jolly Farmers Public House as it appears today.

Breweries: Mrs M Bellamy, Morgan Ales, Steward & Patteson. *Licensees:* Thomas & Thelma Shepherd 1841, John Wilson 1871, William Tuck 1875, Arthur Calver 1917, Edith Calver 1935, Charles King 1936, Cyril Gutteridge. The pub closed in 1962. According to stories handed down generations this old pub was called the Ragged Louse at one time and a resting place for milestone inspectors, more commonly known as tramps. This may or may not be supposition but it certainly was the belief of the last licensee.

The Jolly Farmers was one of the smaller establishments in the village. Ale was served from the barrel as there were no bar or pumps.

1932 at the rear of the Jolly Farmers public house Small Lode Upwell.
Mr. Arthur Calver during his time in the pub trade was licensee of the Horse and Groom, Wheatsheaf and the Jolly Farmers public houses. He also worked some land and was an active member of many village organisations which included the local "lodge" of the Oddfellows.

Arthur Calver, Edith Calver, Margaret Calver, (daughter)

The Wheatsheaf OS NGR TF 4780 0130 March River Side. *(Near to Laddus Drove) Breweries:* Morgan Ales, Steward & Patteson.
Licensees: Robert Nicholas 1851, William Kisby 1881, Arthur Calver 1900, Arnie (Spanker) Green, 1930, Mary Green ran the pub up to the 1950s.

This was another small pub located in a remote area but undoubtedly had a chequered history. Like the Jolly Farmers, ale was drawn from the barrel. From the early 1930s to the 1950s the Wheatsheaf was run by the Green family with Mary Green being the main keeper.
Mrs Tinworth nee Thomlinson lived in the Laddus Drove area during her childhood. She remembers Mr Frank Green, Mary Green's brother, driving a pair of Shire horses from the Wheatsheaf pub to Wiggenhall St Mary Magdalen Fen each day. This amounts to around 14 miles if he took the shortest possible route along the Middle Level Main Drain after joining the river at Morton's Bridge, Outwell. Mr Green owned land in that area where he would do a day's work before setting off for home.
A shire horse could walk little more than four miles per hour so travel time greatly reduced the work that could be done.
We do not have an image of the pub as it was demolished many years ago but we have been assured it had a smart sign outside advertising its existence.

The Wheatsheaf maintained an ale house game that began in the mid 18th century right up to the 1950s called Pitch Penny, Penny Seat or Penny Slot; there were several names to this game. The game was widely played in the Norfolk and Essex public houses.
The game involved tossing a coin across the room and into a hole cut in the seat of a high-backed wooden bench.
There are still a few old farm workers about who remember playing this game in the Wheatsheaf.
The saying and the object of the game was: "As you value your pence, at the hole take your aim. Chuck all safely in, and you'll win the game".
Presumably, one had an amount of coins and the person getting the most through the hole won all that had been thrown.

The Ship later called The **White Hart.** OS NGR TF 505028 High Road.
Brewer: Hogge & Seppings.
Licensees: Samuel Wyatt 1830, John Kay 1836, John Goddard 1851,
George Jarmany 1858. George Jarmany moved to the Horse & Groom.
The White Hart closed soon after the Ecclesiastical Commissioners
purchased it from William Hogge and William Sebbings on 12 Oct
1859 to extend the church burial ground.
Although this public house may be the least known in Upwell, it may
well prove to be one of the most interesting.
It was located in High Road, which begs the question, where is or
where was High Road? Is it reasonable to assume it was somewhere
near the church? The following map, later found in the Norfolk Record
Office confirms our previous research into the location of the White
Hart public house.

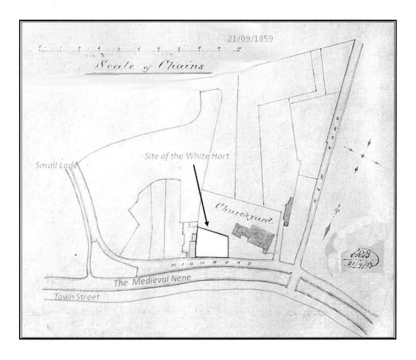

A map found with documents in the Norfolk record office.
A row of Lime trees were planted along the wall soon after this time

Remnants of the White Hart Public house.

This photograph of a partly demolished building taken by Dr Tubbs circa 1859 fits in with the location shown on the map found in the Norfolk record office. The photograph of the church, seen below, was taken some 20 years later by Charles Chapman also illustrates where the pub was located. The church wall, the river and the barn seen in both pictures, validate our research.

C Chapman

A section taken from the map of John Marshall's estate 1807.

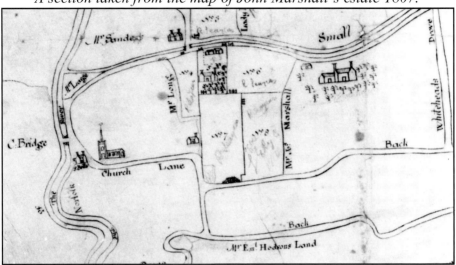

This map was produced before the construction of New Road. The protruding brickwork on both sides of the Old Nene, (now referred to as the Well Creek) supported the original Church Bridge. This bridge gave access to High Road. This brickwork is referred to as being a jetty or landing stage but the structure is not wide enough to support this theory. There is more brickwork recessed into both sides of the river bank that may have been used as a jetty. This should not be confused with the remnant of Mr Smithee's blacksmith shop almost opposite Archway house that is also clearly visible.

Information contained within the map produced to illustrate the property belonging to John Marshall show Church Lane to be located as previously described. This hand drawn map appears to have minor discrepancies when compared with what we see today but the important features are correct.

There can be seen embedded in the wall of the Five Bells car park a large sandstone containing the inscription, *"This wall is the sole property of the rectory and stands upon ground belonging thereto AD1878".* We are of the opinion New Road was constructed around twenty years earlier than this date.

The date has been professionally altered from 1820 to 1878, why?

Could this be the work of a previous owner who may have had a vivid imagination of the village history, perhaps not?

Tubbs/Chapman

This picture of a travelling circus displays a faded image that was thought to be the White Hart public house taken circa 1860. On close inspection the building appears to be the east wing of the Five Bells.

The Five Bells public house faced Church Lane. Church Lane came around this pub to join what is now New Road. The lane turned left and then right at the war memorial, it followed what is called Green Drove or Back Lane before joining the "new road" at Tointons corner. The Drove split at this point. One route went on to Three Holes whilst the other continued towards Tointons Bridge meeting up with Small Lode near Bernard Morton's farm. The route to Three Holes followed an ancient waterway.

The Five Bells OS NGR TF 5054 0275. This public house was originally located in Church Lane, it is now at the New Road, Small Lode Junction.

Breweries: Bagges Brewery of Kings Lynn, This brewery was taken over by Steward & Patteson in 1929, the pub was then owned by Watney Mann, it has been a free house since the 1970s.

Licensees: Thomas Hurst 1830, Mary Hurst 1836, Thomas Hawkins 1845, Thomas Hurst jnr 1875, George Humberstone 1892, William Pruden 1909, Joseph King 1921 to 1926, Abe Hubbard 1926, Louis Turner 1930, Robert (Arnie) Bidwell 1947, Maurice Owen 1953, W Gooch 1958, Edward McGill 1967, Patrick Doran 1973. In the 1980s, the public house was bought from Watney Mann by Mr Eric St. John Foti, the licensees at this time were Patricia and Lesley Banham.

Mr Foti changed the "pub's" name to the Norfolk Punch Health Inn. Mr Foti had earlier taken possession of the old Rectory where he found, stored in a barn, some mid 19th century pews that had been taken out of St. Peter's Church in the 1950s. These pews were installed in the pub and can be seen there today.

The concept of a health establishment did not quite work and the old Five Bells building lay unused for a time. The future of this old pub located in the centre of the village looked bleak until local man Graham Tidmas decided to give it a new lease of life in 1992. There is no doubt the pub was close to being lost to the village at this time. The Five Bells name was rightly re-instated and it became a traditional village pub again. Having saved the pub, Mr Tidmas sold it to Christopher Owen circa 1994.

Village pubs are steeped in history and frequently appear in history chronicles. They were landmarks, and were used as ancient navigation aids similarly to the local church. In modern times when strangers ask for directions inevitably a pub would feature in the conversation.

The names of public houses are historically important to a community, changing them must be questionable.

Since the 1990s, this free house has had a number of owners and tenants. The owners today are Mark and Jane Jones and the tenant is Raghunath Kodakandala.

This image was taken from a postcard sent to Lance Hunter-Rowe during the First World War circa 1915.

The Five Bells seen in the pictures is facing the church. The side entrance that had existed after the closure of Church Lane was discarded; customers accessed the building from a rear door. The curved frontage that can be seen today was added circa 1938.

Tubbs/Chapman

The re-positioning of Church Bridge circa 1855.

The clock, located lower and facing north gives a clue to the date of this photograph which was taken sometime before 1870.

The Five Bells facing the church, is thatched at this time.

THE EARLY PHOTOGRAPHERS

We are particularly grateful to the following gentlemen for capturing many scenes of Upwell, Outwell and the surrounding area from the mid 19th century. We are also fortunate some local people lovingly preserved them over the past hundred and fifty years. It has given us the opportunity to see scenes of the area that would otherwise have been lost forever. Dr William John Tubbs came to Outwell from Parson Drove before settling in Upwell around 1850. He was the "Poor-law Medical Officer" for Outwell and Upwell in the Wisbech Union circa 1852 to 1870. He later lived at Lee House in Upwell which over the years became the home for several doctors. Dr Tubbs gained a reputation for performing serious operations on his patients whilst they were hypnotised. Mesmerism was the latest technology at the time and Dr Tubbs was a keen follower of all the new inventions. Modern photography started around 1839 but accessible glass plate photography came along in 1852. Dr Tubbs embraced this new technology and we are very fortunate to have many examples of his work dating from circa 1854. *More on Dr Tubbs later in this book.*

This may be the oldest birthday card in Upwell.
A present from (picture) Charles Chapman to (picture) William Tubbs on his Birthday Upwell August 3rd 1870 .

This clearly reveals the two men were friends at this time.
The picture is of Dr Tubbs home, Lee House.
Dr Tubbs died just 3 months after getting this card.

William John Tubbs and his second wife Elizabeth

W J Tubbs col

This is possibly the first photograph of St Peter's Church taken circa 1860. The wall between the Five Bells and the church, blocking off Church Lane, would have been quite new at this time.

Mr. Charles Chapman of Walnut House, Upwell was profoundly influenced by Dr Tubbs and continued to record local scenes, some of which will also appear in this publication. We may have considerably more images by Charles Chapman than those taken by Dr Tubbs. It is extremely difficult to say, with any certainty, who to accredit some of the photographs to. I have, with a degree of conjecture, tried to be accurate by using known historic information.

It is likely the two men worked together on many occasions from 1854 up to the time Dr Tubbs died in 1870.

Charles Chapman circa 1860   Mrs Matilda Chapman 1881

Charles and Matilda probably met whilst Matilda was working for her aunt, Elizabeth Smith in the Queens Head.

The quality of these very early pictures is testament to the skills shown by these two local men. The photographs have stood the test of time, something we have yet to prove with modern photography.

Showing the North face of St Peter's Church circa 1890

C Chapman

I am deeply indebted to Christopher Ransome, seen in the picture, for information about his family's history and assisting with research.

We were recently investigating the location of the White Hart public house when we came across the headstone of Charles Chapman.
It was previously thought the grave had been destroyed. Charles Chapman was Christopher's Great Grandfather.

This picture, using Charles Chapman's equipment was taken around 1883. It is probably the earliest image taken of this rail bridge.

Charles Chapmen is observing the new rail bridge at Outwell.

The rail bridge leading to the Outwell goods yard was constructed around 1882-3. It spans the Old Nene and Well Creek near to the intersection with the Wisbech Canal.

Information from Charles Chapman's surviving relatives has revealed he was born with a disability. He travelled around photographing local scenes whilst riding on a variety of machines made by the local blacksmith.

From Outwell Pictorial

The sixty six year old Mr Chapman was in the wrong place at the wrong time on the afternoon of the 14th February 1899 as he was involved in a nasty road accident close to the "Board School" now called the Upwell County Primary School.

A horse and trap being driven by Mrs Louisa Overland, the wife of William John Overland landlord of the Black Bull public house, Upwell collided with him causing him to be "rendered insensible".

Mrs Overland, the female defendant, said on February the 14th she was driving a horse and trap near the school when she saw a "lorry" on the other side of the road coming towards her. The end of the lorry seemed to swing around and into her, she could remember nothing more. Mrs Overland sustained a broken ankle and broken leg.

The accident was fully investigated and reported by PC Pratt, of the Norfolk Constabulary.

Mr Chapman's tricycle was extensively damaged in the collision.

The tricycle was repaired by Mr John William Racey, a blacksmith from Outwell, as reported in the local paper, at a cost of £1 7s 6d but Mr Chapman requested a receipt for £2 10s, illustrating even in those days that some dealings were a little suspect.

John Racey's blacksmith shop Wisbech Road Outwell

It certainly made good business sense to have the Blacksmith and the Sadler's shops side by side on the Wisbech Road Outwell circa 1900. Racey's shop later became one of the first petrol garages in the area and it was owed by Jack Parrott before being sold to John Charles Robb Sr.

Pictured is John W Racy's workshop, from the George Smith col.

Although there are several old wrecks shown in this picture taken around 1900 there appears to be at least one old (sic) "trike" resembling that used by Charles Chapman at the time of his accident.

Charles Chapman suffered from a "contraction of the hip". It was a painful restrictive complaint that preventing him from walking normally.

He was totally dependent on his "tricycle" which he propelled by hand at a speed of around 2 miles per hour.

However this did not prevent him pursuing his great hobby which was a large part of his life up to the time he died on 9 July 1918.

PEOPLE AND COMMERCE

It would be difficult to record all the traders and business people who have trodden the soil of Upwell so I have recorded some for now that have shaped the village in the early days of modern commerce.

There was of course the Townley family who, to this day, still has an influence in selecting our clergymen, albeit perhaps symbolic. William Greaves married the daughter and heiress of Beaupré Bell of Beaupré Hall and took the additional name of Beaupré Bell. *Full Beaupré story in Outwell in a Nutshell.*

Probably the most influential Townley connected to Upwell was the immensely wealthy Richard Greaves Townley *(pronounced Graves, according to the present Richard Townley of Fulbourn),* the older brother to the first Rev. William Gale Townley.

Richard G Townley possessed over 4,000 acres of land in the area, much of it being around the Welney Wash-Land. The Rev. W. G. Townley is credited with the building of the first Welney suspension bridge, replacing the ferryboat. It is likely a crossing has been at this point since the digging of the New Bedford River after the civil war in 1651.

The original Welney Suspension Bridge pictured over the New Bedford River. It was erected in 1824–6 at a cost of £3,000. The bridge was turnpiked in 1827.

The living of the Welney rectory was held by the Townley family, patrons of the mother church, but since 1938 presentations have been made by the Bishop of Ely. Those of Christchurch rectory and Nordelph vicarage were retained by the Townley family.

The church of the Holy Trinity, Nordelph, was erected in 1865 with money it is said, bequeathed by the Rev. William Gale Townley but more likely the Welney suspension bridge and the church were financed by his brother R G Townley, who at that time was Lord of the manor. There is no trace of the church today, it had been neglected and was subsequently demolished in the early 21st century.

Feb 2005

Trinity Church Nordelph has recently been demolished.

The Townley family also contributed greatly towards the building of schools in the area. With an inquisitive mind, one has to question why this family contributed so much towards the education and welfare of the working classes at this particular time.

Historically the gentry were profoundly opposed to educating the poor by denying access to books. Very few people amongst the upper classes made bold moves to advance improvements for the poor.

Yet, it seems in the mid 19th century a family, buried in the heart of an area that had previously been inhospitable to most, suddenly appear to be extremely benevolent! The vast majority of improvements occurred in a 34 year period in the mid 19th century. Between 1831 and 1865, churches and schools were built in Nordelph, Christchurch, Welney, Upwell and Outwell.

The Townley family and their associated ancestors had a profound influence on the area dating from the time of the Conquest (*King William I*) and ended in 1947 with the death of Rev Alexander Peregrine Townley. They hold the advowson *(having the right to nominate someone for a church placement)* of the 13th century church of Upwell, as previously mentioned.

During the mid 19th century, considerable power was firmly in the grip of the Lord of the Manor and the church. The Townley family (locally), at one time, headed both institutions.

Why did they choose the mid 19th century to enhance conditions for the populace when they had the resources to ease the hardship and improve their standard of living many years before?

"Dockie time" Adults and children potato pickers. Upwell circa 1900

The rulers were relatively unconstrained up to this time in our history but circumstances were rapidly changing.

So what, in the mid 19th century, occurred to threaten centuries of tradition to bring about this phenomenal change in attitude towards the lower classes? The industrial revolution was rampant in the north and there were important social changes, neither of which had too much impact on the outer reaches of Fenland at the time.

The aftermath of the Napoleonic wars brought about some improvements for the working classes. Could it have been the increasing popularity of the non-conformist? The Methodist movement, started by John Wesley in the mid 18th century offered more to ordinary people than the conventional church, with fewer constraints.

When John Wesley died in 1791, he was arguably the most popular man in the country. The Wesley movement exploded after his death. His "Method" of preaching Christianity was being embraced by such people as John Newton and William Wilberforce who were instrumental in the abolition of slavery. Wesley was deeply opposed to slavery and vehemently supported the working classes. The non-conformist church rapidly increased in popularity during the mid 19th century and touched even the smallest community. Influence and power were changing. Under Wesley's direction, Methodists became leaders in many social issues of the day.

The village working classes were being allowed access to schools *(Methodist Sunday schools)* and had books that were readily available. Businessmen were deserting the conventional church to join the Wesley movement. The "Methodist" ministers, controversially, read the bible in English, as opposed to Latin, which was read in the conventional church. Links to Rome had been severed by the founder of the Church of England for almost 300 years.

Seating was allocated on a first come first served basis with no "pew fees" to pay. In the conventional church the poor were not allowed to sit without payment even if seats were empty.

Paradoxically, Richard G Townley financed the installation of the galleries and filled the aisle with pews in St. Peter's church at this time.

Was the building of schools and churches in these remote villages an attempt to emulate the non-conformists and reduce the threat to the conventional church? Perhaps not, but we do know most ordinary village folk led a miserable existence whilst a few were living a lavish lifestyle up to the mid 19th century.

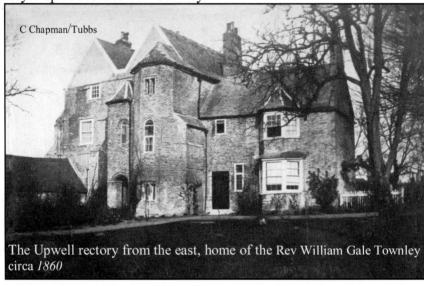

C Chapman/Tubbs

The Upwell rectory from the east, home of the Rev William Gale Townley circa *1860*

Beaupré Hall.   Belonging to R G Townley *1827*

Upwell Hall — Built for the Rev George J Huddleston

◆━━━━━◆

PEOPLE

A School Board of 5 members was formed in 1874: James Webber, Clerk to the board. Edward James Hugh Waudby, registrar of births & deaths for Upwell sub-district. Upwell Public Hall Co Limited (W Ollard, chairman, F T Ollard, clerk). Henry West Hartley, Public hall keeper, town crier and bill poster. James D. Digby, sec National Skating Association. Lister Swann M.R.C.V.S. veterinary surgeon, chairman of Upwell Hall and Upwell & Outwell Gas Co. Limited. Clerk was William Welchman and R Dales, James Webber, Solicitor, commissioner for oaths in the Supreme Court & clerk to the school board, clerk to manager's national school and to the Charity trustees, Upwell (Isle of Ely), Upwell (Norfolk) and of Outwell, working from Bridge buildings Wisbech. Welchman & Carrick, solicitors at 9 Crescent, Wisbech.

William Welchman. (Welchman & Carrick) solicitors. Commissioners for taking affidavits, clerk to the Level of Upwell, Welney, Needham burial & Birdbeck district. They were also solicitors to the Upwell & Outwell Gas Co. Limited.
Insurance agents: Law Union, J Webber. Norwich Union Fire, James H Inman. Norwich & London Accident & Phœnix, Alfred John Elworthy, Royal Exchange, J F Balding & C S Elworthy.

Prominent Upwell residents 1883:
Chapman Charles, Walnut Tree house, Rev. Robert David Cowan Russell B.A. (curate), Walter Berry, surgeon, medical officer & public vaccinator, Lode house. Rev John Beauvoir Dalison, M A. J P. The Rectory. Miss Elger, Edward Harwin, William Lee, John Charles Osborn, Miss Berry, Walter Berry, Rev. Joseph Brown, (Baptist) Mrs Hanslip Palmer, Lister Swann, James Webber, William Welchman, Henry West, Samuel West.
Norfolk Farmers:
John Beckett, John Bowers, farmer & market gardener, Thomas Bowers., William Bradley, William John Burgess, John Carter. Joseph Dales, John Delph, farmer & poulterer, John Esgate, Mrs. Frederick Frusher, Frederick Billett Green, William James Green, John Hall, farm bailiff to John Cabread Jones esq. Matthew Hawkins, Jeremiah Hill, John James, Edward Mason Lister, James Lister, Abraham Means, jun. George Watton Melton, Benjamin Notson Milk, George Naylor, Robert Minson Plumb, artificial manure agent & potato farmer. William Rogers, Samuel Shepherd, George Swann, Aaron Tuck, William Turner, Charles Welbourn, John Wiles, farmer & landowner. Thomas Whitehead, farmer & carrier.
Farmers Isle of Ely:
William Berry, (Mrs) George Bliss, William Brown, White Lion & farmer, James Boyce Tip's End, James Dalton Tip's End, Elworthy, Green Christopher, William Headin, Jonathan Lock, Henry William John Fosbrooke Ream, James Thomas Thistleton, William Watson, Samuel West, Henry West, jun. Henry West. William Pethero, farmer & landowner, & potato merchant.

Carpenter & Wheelwright:
John Osborn, Philip Tombleson, Edgar Everson, builder & wheelwright.
Harry Goodman. George W Filby, carpenter. John May, carpenter.
Benjamin Webber carpenter. Jarvis John, carpenter & builder.
Blacksmith/Ferrier:
Baker James Morton, William Knowles, John Balding Smithee.
Grocer & Draper:
James Henry Inman, grocer, draper & agent to W. & A. Gilbey, wine &
spirit merchants & post office. William Bradfield, Edward C Barnes,
Nathaniel Cragg, John Fillenham, tailor, Miss Rebecca Stevens, dress
maker, George Hunt, tailor, John Butler, tailor. Mrs Jane Oliver, baker
& confectioner, Mrs Mary Ann Searle, shopkeeper.

Mrs Mary Searle's shop (1883) was located almost opposite Church Bridge, to the left, and adjacent to the first Upwell pharmacy.

Beer Retailer:
Arthur Inman Wilcock, ale, stout & coal merchant, William Felstead, John Judd, John Maywood, William Tuck, Mrs Ann Jarmany, William Kirby.
Butcher:
William White, Mrs Susan Ward, Joseph Beckett, butcher & gasfitter. J T Spikings, Valentine Townley, grocer & butcher. T Elworthy.
Boot / Shoe maker:
Henry jun. Pleasants, boot & shoe maker. James Muley, boot & shoe maker. William Mason, boot maker, Philip Bridgeman, shoe maker. Henry Tuck, shoe maker. George Marsh, shoe maker.
Brick layer:
James Parker, John Fisher Hammond, James Sutton, William Sutton.
Miscellaneous:
Elworthy A. & C. auctioneer & appraisers, house & land agents at 4 Exchange square, Wisbech. Roger Stone, market gardener.
William Warby, steam threshing machine owner. Fisher Rowlett, cattle dealer. Marshall Forth, miller (wind). Joseph Beckett, butcher & gasfitter. Henry Bickley, hair dresser. George Brewin, watch maker & furniture dealer. William Goulding, chemist. Mrs Susannah Jakens baker. William Mayhew, plumber & glazier. Charles Overland, plumber & glazier. Thomas Shepherd, steam & wind miller & corn factor. John Warby, farmer & thrashing machine proprietor.

1896. Upwell Norfolk. Gents.
Rev. Arthur Charles (Baptist). Charles Chapman Walnut Tree House, Dalison Rev: John Beauvoir M.A., J.P. Rectory. Gibbon John George M.D. Mrs McGloch, Mrs Oliver, Mrs Thistleton, Rev.
Thompson, William Craig B.A. (curate), Miss Truman Brackeburgh. John George Gibbon MD, physician & surgeon.

COMMERCIAL.
James Morton, Baker. John Bekett, Blacksmith. Joseph Beckett Farmer. Thomas Beckett, Butcher. William Bradley, Farmer. Thomas Bowers, Farmer. Thomas Coote & Son, Coal merchants. William Cox, Farmer. Joseph Dales, Coal merchant. John Deptford, Farmer & carrier.

Elworthy & Son, Auctioneers & Builders, (Wisbech) Charles Elworthy, Farmer & landowner. John Esgate, Farmer. George William Filby, Carpenter. John Fillenham, Tailor. Thomas Forth, Miller (wind). Alfred Frusher, Farmer, Pingle Farm. Frederick Frusher, Farmer. Robert Frusher, Farmer. Hy Goodman, Carpenter & Wheelwright. George Goodyear, Farmer. Frederick Billet Green, Farmer. William Hardy, Huddleston Arms P.H. Henry West Hartley, Town crier, Bill poster, Public hall keeper & School attendance officer. William Eli, Butcher. Thomas William Hines, Stone mason. George Hircock, Shopkeeper. Humberston George, Five Bells, Commercial hotel & posting house. Arthur Wilcock, Farmer. James William, Farmer. Wilby Watson Jarvis, Carpenter. Joseph Lawrence, Beer retailer. Joseph Laughlin, Grocer. Charles Lawton, farmer. Job May, Beer retailer.

Abraham Means, Jun. farmer. George Henry Melton, farmer. George Watton Melton, farmer. Milk Benjamin Notson, farmer. James Mulley, boot & shoe maker. Charles Murfin, farm bailiff to John Cabread Jones esq. George Naylor, farmer. Joseph Osborne, grocer. Charles Overland, Rose & Crown P.H. William Overland, beer retailer. James Parker, builder. Henry Pleasants, boot & shoemaker. Rt. Minson Plumb, artificial manure agent. Stephen Searl, farmer. Samuel Shepherd, farmer. Thomas Shepherd, saddler & harness maker & at Outwell William George Shepherd, miller (steam & wind)

Stevens & Son, grocers. Miss Rebecca Stevens, dress maker. James Sutton, bricklayer. Richard Sutton, bricklayer. George Swann, farmer. Ernest Albert Thorpe, baker. Thomas Tointon, farmer. Jacob Tombleson, farrier. Alfred Turner, farmer. Billney James Turner, farmer. Upwell Public Hall Co, Limited (Wm. Welchman, clerk) Frederick Vawser, rate collector & registrar of births & deaths for Upwell sub-district. Jarvey Walker, farmer. James Warby, farmer John Warby, farmer. William Warby, steam thrashing and machine owner. Frederick Ward, beer retailer. John Ward, Black Horse P.H. Joseph Webb, miller. (wind) Haddon William Webber, bricklayer. Thomas White, farmer. William White, farmer. John Wiles, farmer.

1896. Upwell Isle of Ely (Cambs)
Misses Berry. Rev. Joseph Brown (Baptist). James Elliott Jameson, B.A. M.B. Thomas Ernest Price. Webber James, William Welchman. Henry West J.P. Samuel West.
Commercial 1896 continued:
Allott William Aaron, M.R.C.V. S. veterinary surgeon, Upwell Hall. Thomas Andrews, farmer, Francis James Balding, estate & insurance agent. John Balding Smithee, blacksmith. Peter Bliss, farmer, Henry Blunt jun farmer. Charles Blithe, butcher. James Boyce, farmer, (Tip's end). Wm Brown, White Lion P.E. & farmer. Nathaniel Cragg, grocer, Thos James Dolton. Farmer. (Tip's end) Elworthy & Son, auctioneers & appraisers, house, land & estate agents at 4 Exchange square Wisbech. Frederick William Fillenham, tailor, John Hammond Fisher, bricklayer, Gibbon & Jameson, surgeons, William Gouldin chemist & agent for W & A Gilbey Limited, wine & spirit merchants. William Green, farmer, William Griffin, grocer, & draper, William Headin, farmer, Jeremiah Hills, farmer, Thomas William Hines, stone & marble. Mason. *(Tragically killed near Outwell Church)*

Located between the old Queens Head & the builders yard.

George Hunt, tailor, Henry James Inman, grocer & draper, Post office. Mrs Priscilla Jakens, baker. William James, grocer & draper. Elliott James Jameson BA. MB. B. Ch. Surgeon. John Johnson, baker. Robert Johnson, beer retailer. James Lister, farmer. George Marsh, shoe maker. Immanuel William Mayhew, plumber & glazier. John Maywood, beer retailer. Mrs Rachael Oldfield, shopkeeper. Charles Overland, plumber & glazier. James Overland Old Duke's Head P.H. Ernest Thomas Price L.R.C.P. & S. Edin. L.F.P. & S.Glas. Surgeon, medical officer & public vaccinator, No. 11 District, Wisbech Union. Mrs Ann Mary Rallison, Queen's Head P.H. John Fosbrooke Ream, farmer. William George Shepherd, Wind miller & corn factor. Isaac Smith, poulterer. John Thomas Spikings, butcher. William Sutton, builder. Valentine Townley, shopkeeper & butcher. Tuck Henry, shoe maker.

Upwell Public Hall Co, Lim. (William Welchman, clerk). Upwell & Outwell Gas Co. Limited (R. Dales, chairman; William Welchman, clerk). Frederick Vawser, registrar of births & deaths for Upwell sub-district, Wisbech union.

Watson William, farmer, Tip's End. Webber James, solicitor commissioner for oaths in the Supreme Court; perpetual commissioner for taking acknowledgments of married women in the county of Cambridgeshire, clerk to the school board, clerk to managers 'Outwell National school, to charity trustees, Upwell, Norfolk & of Outwell.

Welchman, Carrick & Jackson, solicitors & at 13 South brink, Wisbech. Welchman William (firm, Welchman, Carrick & Jackson), solicitor & commissioner for oaths, coroner for Isle of Ely, clerk to the Level of Upwell, Outwell, Denver & Welney, to the Needham burial & Birdbeck district, clerk to the Upwell & Outwell Gas co. Limited, clerk to the Public Hall Co. Limited, clerk to Upwell Isle charity trustees at Wisbech. Henry West, farmer & landowner, land agent & valuer. Henry West, Jun. farmer. Samuel West, farmer & landowner.

COMMERCE (20th century)

W.J. Fillenham started his tailoring business in his mother's house sited near Pious Drove almost opposite the British Legion Hall. He used her front room as his workshop and conducted sales from the house. As his business progressed he was able to move to larger premises opposite Church Bridge, now called the Bridal Shop. Later, he had a house built near his mother's house and called it "Riverdale", this house and his mother's are still standing. His mother's old house still has one front window larger than the other allowing in the required light and indicating the room where the business started.

On moving to the larger shop at Church Bridge he expanded into retailing gents, ladies and children's clothes but retained his tailoring business in a large upstairs room at the back of the building. He employed two tailors, a Mr Jim Faulks and Mr John Wilson who did all the sewing. Mr Fillenham remained the pattern cutter. Mr. Wilson claimed that any buttons he sewed on a suit would never come off during the owner's lifetime.   Mr. Fillenham retired towards the latter part of the Second World War through ill health and moved to Wisbech, he lived to the age of 100. The shop was taken over by Miss Eggett and Mr Jack Francis.

Mr. Frederick (Ernie) Johnson started his business at the age of 21 after taking over a small shop in the early 1930's previously owned by Mrs. Griffin. This small shop in Town Street is now known as the post office, Mr. Ernest Johnson was born at Green Drove Upwell.
just seven regular customers when Mr. Johnson commenced trading. His first task was to clear all the old stock, which included items dating back to the First World War. In an effort to gain trade he set off on his bicycle around the village to deliver goods and canvass for more customers.

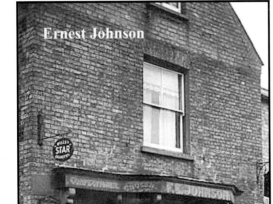

Ernest Johnson

As business increased he was able to purchase a car and later a van. He was forced to increase the size of his premises so bought the property next but one to the little shop and traded for 40 years. Ernie Johnson served as a special constable gaining many awards for long service. By 1973 Mr. Johnson had retired due to ill heath and sold his business as a thriving going concern to Mrs. S.M. Davis of Essex.

Ernie Johnson was involved with local activities all his life being chairman, president, treasurer and secretary of Upwell Town Football Club for over 60 years. Mr. Johnson was also chairman of Upwell Men's Institute, secretary of the village bowls club and a member of the playing field committee.

<u>William (Bill) Brighty</u>, Bill was a potato merchant's son and was born in 1927 at the Dovecote Upwell, he lived at Kendor House during his early years. On leaving school he worked for his father but thought his pay packet of ten shillings a week was not enough to make progress in life. He then took on a bricklaying apprenticeship with Mr. Youngs but soon left, as his wages were half of what his father gave him. He returned to working for his father who also owned a farm at Downham Market. His next job was working for Mr. Jimmy Russell in the early 1940s. He was a cattle dealer and fruit grower. Also working for Mr. Russell at that time was another well-known Upwell man called "Puff" Bell.

Bill was called up to serve in the R.A.F but took early release to start his first business, which was egg production.

Bill and his wife Lena had lived at New Road and Listers Drove before purchasing property at St. Peters Road previously owned by Mr. Hardy. During his retirement Bill lived in his new house next to the paper shop on the crescent.

William Brighty

The Brighty's contract pea harvesting business is one of the largest in the area. His enormous, purpose built machines have been a familiar sight on the Fenland fields for many years.

<u>Mr Jack Stittle</u> was born 1893 in Newmarket the home of horse racing. So it was little surprise that he followed the family tradition by learning the saddler and harness maker trade from his father starting at the age of 14. We have to remember that to become a top tradesman at this type of work takes years to build up the physical requirements. The strength needed in the fingers is enormous and of course the human skin has to be like the materials being worked, which can only be achieved through years of hard work. He later tried his luck at football before the First World War, playing for teams such as Boston, Worksop and Chesterfield. After the war he moved to Upwell and worked for Mr J. Hircock whose shop was sited near to what is now the fish and chip shop. About 1925 he set up his own business in Workhouse Lane, making all the equipment required by the many horses that were around in those days. He continued playing football for Wisbech and later Upwell Town until about 1930.

In the mid 1950s the changing face of farming forced skilled craftsmen such as Jack Stittle to seek other merchandise to manufacture. The rapid decline of the humble shire-horse and the emergence of the tractor meant equipment made from leather was no longer required. His skill with working the leather made the transition easy for him as he produced school satchels and handbags by the hundreds. It is thought he made over 3,000 handbags before finally retiring at the age of 78. If it could be made from leather Jack Stittle could make it.

One small job led to an enormous undertaking in the late 1950s. He made a particularly good job of dog collars. The strong stiff leather face, the ornate brass stud decorations and the neatly hand sewn soft leather backing strips made them extremely desirable. But what the male fashion conscious brigade noticed was, many pop stars of the day were wearing belts similar to these dog collars with the studs spelling out a name on the belt. No self-respecting rocker would be seen in town without a studded leather belt round his trousers! Mr Stittle could not satisfy the demand for belts, he certainly never got into a position where he could make them or anything else for stock. In later life he made briefcases and occasionally repaired the shop bought light harnesses. He often would proudly say "Nothing I have made has ever been brought back to me for repair". That's the hallmark of a top craftsman.

Jack Stittle repairing a shire-horse's collar in his Upwell workshop.

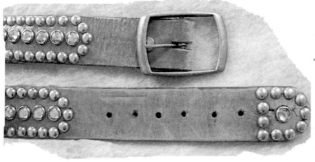

This is a typical studded belt made for the fashion conscious ladies.

The men's belts were usually much wider.

93

Jack Stittle

Below: JE Hircock. Saddler and harness maker in Town Street (Now called School Rd) with a very young Jack Stittle.

During the recent past, a time we could call "modern history", there have been many traders and businesses in Upwell. It would be very difficult to list them all in great detail at one time. It is the intention to record as many as it is practically possible in the ensuing publications during the next few years.

James William (Billy) Sutton started work as a butcher's apprentice for Eli Henfrey in 1906 at the age of twelve. After serving time in France as a butcher and cook during the First World War, he started his own business in Thurlands Drove. He did his own slaughtering in an open fronted hovel. Slaughtering was part of a butcher's trade and common practice up to the 1950s.

The old hovel used for the slaughtering soon became too small for the work Billy was taking on with his rapidly expanding business. In 1923 he built a purpose built slaughterhouse, shop and a residential house in School Road, formerly Town Street. The new site became the prime slaughterhouse for the local cattle and pig dealers. The business employed a skilled slaughter-man, six men and of course Billy's son Derek, who since leaving school, had been taught the business. Derek took over the business in 1950.

In 1959 Derek Sutton purchased the premises belonging to Joseph King near Church Bridge. The premises had been used by four previous butchers including the successful Spikings family, who now trade at St. Peter's Road Upwell.

This ancient property as it stood, did not suit Derek's ambitious innovative plans for a modern butcher's shop.

Late 1959 the building was substantially refurbished, the new shop included a refrigerated window and store room. The "shops" interior was fitted with white tiles, a new counter and modern display cabinets.

Mr Brian Tweed started his career with Frederick Stokes of Manea. He was employed by Derek Sutton in 1959 to manage the new shop. Brian worked at the Sutton's School Road shop for around six months whilst the new shop was being refurbished. The new "lock up" shop was opened to the public Tuesday 9 February 1960. The building block also contained an insurance office and a residential house at this time.

After the death of Mr Derek Sutton, Brian Tweed purchased the shop including the attached buildings in 1964.

Above: The shop as it stood during the time of Joseph King pre 1959.
Below: During the 1959 refurbishments.

The interior of the new shop 1960

Brian Tweed was the shop manager in 1960.

The property was further upgraded in 1974 when Mr Tweed
amalgamated the three buildings to produce what can be seen today.

2009

Circa 1965

PEOPLE

Mrs. Janet Smith was the daughter of the local chemist Thomas Hill, she married and lived at Dodd's Stile. At one time she owned the Upwell Village Hall and her son Donald owed the sports field. The family were generous benefactors to the village. Janet Smith was a keen local historian and collected anything connected to Upwell, in later life she lived in Stowlangtoft Hall Nursing Home near Bury St. Edmunds. When in her 80s, she wrote a piece for a local magazine that informs us of the things we no longer have around us.

She was a good friend of Muriel Byton who gave me the original script in 1995. I will quote from her notes as she intended them to be read.

"Many things have gone from the village from the time there was no electricity, no water supplied to the houses. Water was taken by the pipes in the gutters to a brick built cistern and the water was either by pump or a bucket let down on the end of a pole. The village pump standing by the Five Bells Hotel was very useful. Gone is the Smithy that stood by the riverside opposite Archway House, and the garden by the river, large enough to grow fruit trees and vegetables. The last one outside Mr. Brian Tweed's shop had two large yew trees that were years old. The parish rooms, which were then called the Institute, were used by the men to play cards, dominoes and read the newspapers. Miss Kate Elgen, the church organist who kept a school for girls where we wrote in copybooks and wrote our sums on a slate with a very squeaky pencil, used the other part. The Upwell Fair was held in the summer with stalls by the riverside where one could buy sticks of striped rock, or small toys and china ornaments. There was a small roundabout on the land in front of the church, worked by hand and a larger one in the yard of the Five Bells worked by a pony trotting round the middle. The "Passing Bell" which was one of the church bells, rang when there was a death in the village, it sounded three times for a man, twice for a woman and finally rang the number of years of age.

The bath-night was an event. Water had to be heated in a large copper, carried upstairs and of course carried down again. There was no water in the house that meant no flushing toilets. That meant a short walk down the garden when necessary to a small building for that purpose.

There was a bakery next to the opening by the chemist shop, which was kept by Mr. William Gouldin and my father Thomas Hill. On Saturday night the fires were let out and the heat was just right for the people who lived in nearby cottages to bring their Sunday joint to cook in the oven. I was able to see them as my house was behind the chemist shop. There were barges on the river loaded with coal and peat, drawn by a horse on the towpath and led by a man who had to walk till the barges reached Outwell. "Oh there are many things to remember!"

We will never record all the social history of our villages. So much is lost with the passing of time. Janet Smith died in 1993 aged 99.

Mrs Bothamley and Mrs Janet Smith in top hat, at Dodd's stile in 1938

<u>Mrs. Muriel Byton</u> recalls some interesting stories about her father Sidney Bertram Stocks born 1895, who was a native of Upwell. His aunt, Susan Lawson and his guardian Sarah Warby brought him up. They lived in a small cottage on School Road that was later owned by Robert (Bob) Godfrey. As a young man he was employed by Dr Reynolds as a chauffeur who practised at the New Bridge surgery and lived at New Bridge House, he also lived at Lee House at one time. Dr Reynolds had always had a desire to drive himself so he asked Mr. Stocks to teach him.

They decided to drive along the sixteen-foot river as it was long and straight but after a short time Mr. Stocks asked the doctor to stop as he was concerned they were about to end the journey in the water. The doctor said, "Stocks what is wrong with you", "I would rather walk home" said Mr. Stocks. You will have us both drowned, "Well I suppose you had better drive home then" said the doctor. Educated as he was, Dr. Reynolds never did manage the art of driving a car.

After his marriage to Alice, Bert lived in a small cottage near Tointons Road and worked for the rector the Rev. A.P. Townley as chauffeur and gardener.

He often won prizes exhibiting fruit, vegetables and other crops in the annual summer produce show in Mr. Walter Hunter-Rowe's cold store opposite the vicarage gardens where they were grown. The Rev Townley was particularly fond of fresh herbs and spices that were grown in his garden at the rectory, having studied their origins for many years. When the Rev. Townley retired, Bert rented a small wooden workshop owned by the Horn brothers in Town Street that was previously a blacksmith's shop, and repaired cycles, radios and charged up the accumulators. The accumulator was an early form of battery used to power the radio.

Mr & Mrs Stocks

During the last war Mr Stocks was an Upwell postman usually on the Small Lode round. His daughter helped out with delivering the post. The postmaster at this time was Mr. Payne. Mr. Stocks was a proud Upwell man through and through, he was well known and respected by all the villagers.

Trivia: Small Lode, a waterway that was almost certainly cut during Roman times to assist with the transportation of peat from Walsingham Fen. Peat was very much a sought after commodity by the Romans. Walsingham Fen stretches from the Pingle, Middle Level main Drain to the Aqueduct then almost reaches Nordelph. The waterway connected to the Old Nene almost opposite to Ransome's Close to the east and the Well Creek to the west, opposite (sic) Molycourt Road Outwell. The Lode forked at the Pingle with a branch heading south-east, perhaps as far as Harwins Farm. The peat might have travelled along Well Stream to be off-loaded near West's Farm Christchurch where the Well Stream ran alongside the Roman Causeway.

The Great Fen Project revealed the peat workings but local farmers have been aware of the vast peat deposits in this location for centuries. Following the stubble and reed burning, it was not unusual in the 1950s for peat to burn underground for days. As a child, I remember watching the firemen struggling to contain the fires. The fires were sometimes left to burn themselves out. The waterway at Small Lode was filled with household waste in the late 1950s and early 1960s.

<u>Mr. Eric St. John Foti's</u> unusual name is a combination of English and Sicilian. He came to Upwell in the 1970s and purchased the old rectory, a building that had been occupied by the Townley family for around 150 years. It was at this time, the old rectory was renamed Welle Manor Hall by Mr Foti, the rectory had previously been named Sanford House. Mr. Foti stirred mixed feelings amongst the locals, as he appeared to possess an unusual talent for discovering long lost relics hidden for hundreds of years. I have to confess I have found it difficult to authenticate some of the claims that were made during his time in Upwell. Mr Foti was well known for producing a drink called "Norfolk Punch". According to Mr. Foti none other than Barbara Cartland gave it her support. The published advertising for the drink claimed to have links with the 13th century. There are many knowledgeable historians who have raised an eyebrow at the suggestion.

There can be no argument about Mr Foti's ability to generate interest in local history and he certainly was an astute businessman.

Questions might be asked why Mr. Eric St. John Foti should have a place in a book about the history of Upwell.

One has to admire this gentleman as he did create employment for the area and refurbished parts of the village that were in decline.

The name "Norfolk" Punch raised the national prominence of this small Norfolk village as did Mr Foti with his imaginative interpretations of the local history. In addition to the old Rectory, he purchased the old chapel, The Five Bells public house and the Village Hall all of which received much needed investment.

In 1994 the brand and factory were bought by Orchard Drinks of Hartlepool and production transferred to Hartlepool. Then in 2000, Orchard Drinks was bought by Britvic.

Mr. Foti moved from Upwell and started another enterprise near Downham Market called "Collector's World". Collector's world and Norfolk Punch no longer exist although recent research suggests this non-alcoholic drink is soon to be on sale once more.

In 1883, the public officers were selected during the vestry meeting under the overseer, the Rev John Beauvoir Dalison. It was to be the final meaningful vestry meeting. During this meeting the following were appointed:
Alfred John Elworthy, surveyor and accountant, assistant overseer and collector of poor rate for Upwell and income tax collector for Upwell and Welney. Registrar of Births & Deaths, for Upwell sub-district. Edward James and Hugh Waudby Police Sergeant, William Bennyworth, Walter Berry, Medical Officer & Public Vaccinator (11 & 12 districts Wisbech Union and 2nd district Downham Union).

The elected public officers on Church Bridge circa 1883

PUBLIC OFFICERS

Parish councils were formed in England under the 1894 Local Government Act to take over local civic duties in villages across the country. Before this date a variety of groups based around ecclesiastical parishes had responsibility for village matters, in a system of local government that came from the feudal system started by William the Conqueror. The feudal system was orchestrated by monarchs, lords, landowners and later the church leaders. The meetings were held in the vestry by order of the local vicar before 1894.

Upwell, like most communities were historically governed by the Lords of the Manor (the Beaupré family) who were awarded land by various ruling monarchs and instructed to control the populace. They were responsible for working the land collecting taxes and making certain law and order was adhered to no matter how harsh or one sided that may be. The local priest, who at one time was catholic, had much power up to the dissolution of the monasteries. After the dissolution, the church became the most powerful ruling body, often in collaboration with the Lord of the Manor and other privileged land owners. I have used the word collaboration because history has shown in many cases the peasants were often hideously discriminated against and in the main not encouraged to be independent. In fact the under classes had very few rights and were often severely punished simply for showing interest in such things as a book or means of communication other than by word of mouth.

By the Year 1601, "Church Vestry" Meetings were so organised and workable that it was quite natural for legislators to give them the responsibility of levying the poor rate. These were the first effective local taxes. Everyone in the parish was entitled to attend Church Vestry Meetings but in practice the work fell to a few individuals rather like parish councils as we know them today.

The vestry meetings were regarded as important in that they decided who would police the village for the coming year by appointing the constables, overseers and others under the guidance and in most cases instruction of the local church minister. Although parishioners had a right to attend the vestry meetings, in truth, few outside the elite bothered, as any words uttered often brought retribution. At the toll of the church bell, local dignitaries would muster in the vestry to debate issues affecting the village. The minister may have attended depending on the importance of the meeting, he certainly was aware of what issues were being discussed and made his feelings known. He was obliged to attend the meetings that required collecting the parish subscriptions. Disagreeing with his views was not a wise thing do.

The church was still powerful up to 1894 but the 1847 "Rectories Act" was the beginning of authority being given to ordinary parishioners. The law stated the populace should attend church but by the early 19th century, alternative places of worship were springing up all over the country. Many ardent church followers preferred to support the "nonconformists", thus further reducing the church status.

The church remained responsible for collecting ten per cent of all earnings from the land, a practice that existed in one form or another up to 1977.

In 1538, Henry VIII dissolved the Abbey at Ramsey. The Beaupre family became the new patrons, having no male progeny, the patronage descended through the female line to the Bell family. William Greaves married Elizabeth Bell, heiress of Beaupré Bell of Beaupré Hall Outwell he took the additional names of Beaupré Bell.

The patronage descended to the Townley family, Richard Townley's only surviving son, Richard Greaves Townley. He was born in 1751 and educated at Rochdale, Eton, Manchester Grammar School, Trinity College, Cambridge and the Middle Temple. He married Margaret Gale in 1785. On the death of his great-uncle William Greaves Beaupré Bell in 1787 he inherited his entire estate, including Beaupré Hall and Fulbourn Manor near Cambridge where the Townley family continues to live today.

More recent: <u>Mr Leslie Peacock</u> was elected on the Upwell Norfolk parish council just after the Second World War and served for 41 years. He retired in October 1998 and was presented with an engraved walking stick from the council chairman Mr. Hugh Beckett.

The Upwell Salvation Army Hall dates from 1883

<u>Mr Harry Hancock</u>, the well known corn merchant lived in Upwell almost all his life. He learned his trade whilst working for Mr Hutson and Messrs Kenny and Co. He took over their business around 1930. He was later assisted by his son Ernie when he managed a bit of leave from the army during WWII.

They bought the abandoned Salvation Army hall and expanded the business but sadly Harry died in 1944 at the age of 74. Ernie was allowed out of the army to take over the business. The business was further expanded, to supply all manner of goods to the farming fraternity. Ernie Hancock's business became an integral part of Upwell. On Ernie's retirement the business was taken over by Dennicks of Wisbech. The Upwell business eventually closed but Dennicks continued to trade from Wisbech. Sidney Banks took over the granary after Dennicks. The old hall took on a different role when it was then bought by Gerald Harnwell of "Harnwell Electrical".

Ernie Hancock died June 1994.

The Hunter-Rowe Family. During many presentations to the good folk of Outwell and Upwell over the years I have often told a story about when I joined the army. The story starts when I needed a suitcase so I borrowed two chitting trays from Mr. Lance Hunter-Rowe's orchard. I nailed two door hinges down one edge and bailer twine on the other, for a handle! I knew if I had lost the case it would be returned as it had an Upwell address stamped down the sides. Of course that was just a story. In reality if I really did need a suitcase and I had approached Mr Hunter-Rowe I have no doubt he would have given me money for one. Such was the man that gave an enormous amount to villages over many years.

Other members of this family gave similarly. They were an extremely successful business family and provided much needed employment within their fruit growing business and other enterprises. Mr Hunter-Rowe, one of nine children, lived at "Redroofs", Town Street Upwell until he moved to Shouldham Hall Nursing Home where he died in January 1985 at the fine age of 90.

It is not known just how many gifts he and his family donated to the villages but the ones I have been able to find out about demonstrate just how generous this family was. The Hunter-Rowe Family financed much of the school building of the Bethel Chapel Outwell (later to be the workshop for Mr. Colin Brown) including paying for the entire roof just after the turn of the 20th century. Donations were received by Upwell Secondary Modern School for several projects including the swimming pool, enabling the school to be the first secondary school to have its own swimming pool. It has to be said that the pupils and staff also contributed greatly towards the pool.

Mr L Hunter-Rowe subscribed to the footbridge over the Well Creek near the Pious Drove junction.

He bestowed substantial amounts to establishments and organisations such as the Health Centre, the Royal British Legion and the Well Creek Trust. Without his assistance, the preservation of this old waterway might have been unattainable.

It would be accurate to say this man was a doer! He was not content to simply sit on committees and attend meetings. He made sure improvements were carried out, he believed in contributing and encouraged others to act likewise. He gained great respect from all he had dealings with. He certainly involved himself in the community, being Alderman of the Town Council, and he represented the Isle of Ely until its amalgamation with Cambridgeshire. He was a member of the County Highways Committee, a trustee of Upwell and District Independent Order of Oddfellows, a member of the Agricultural Committee and served on the North Cambridgeshire Hospital Management Committee, being at one time vice-chairman. He had connections with the "Organisation for the Blind" and he served on the Parish Council for 30 years, during which time he was chairman. He was a member of the Advisory Committee on which he advised on the purchase of the Bowthorpe Hospital Wisbech and Glenfield House Residential Home. During the First World War Mr. Hunter-Rowe served in the army with the Royal Field Artillery. He later joined the Second Leinster Regiment, where he spent 12 months in the trenches until he was wounded at Ypres. An unusual souvenir from the 1914-1918 war kept by Mr. Hunter-Rowe was a biscuit that seemed to stay in good condition for 60 years. He was chairman of the Beaupré School Governors from 1939 when the school opened, to 1971.

Mr. Stanley Booley, Headmaster of the school paid tribute to him by saying. "We will never again see the likes of this man in these villages".
Left:
Mr L Hunter-Rowe, Mr Booley, Mrs Hunter-Rowe. 1949

His brothers William and Walter also donated considerable funds to many very worthwhile projects like homes for the aged and several similar establishments on the Norfolk coast.

Mr William Gray

I have been fortunate enough to know Don and Anne Frusher practically all my life, particularly Anne, who was working at Beaupré School when I was a child. They have been instrumental in much of my research into the modern history of Upwell. Anne's father, <u>Mr William Gray</u> was the chauffeur to Mr William Welchman, the local solicitor who lived at Birbeck House. Birbeck House existed on the site of the present day Methodist Chapel. Mr Gray lived in the cottage next door. During one of my many chats with the Frushers, a story about this car cropped up.

A good friend, Mr Arthur Scott of Elm, told me a very sad story about one of his relatives having an accident with the Wisbech to Upwell Tram many years ago. He was uncertain of the date and the precise circumstances but the story enthralled me so much that I did a little research.

The following was reported in the local newspaper.

On the 25 April 1914 a horse-drawn trap being driven by Mr Frank Scott was travelling towards Boyce's Bridge, opposite Dial House.
The horse became restive and backed the trap into the path of the approaching tram. The locomotive driver was unable to stop the tram in time to prevent a collision. In the ensuing melee, one of the cart's wheels was torn off. Mrs Elizabeth Scott was thrown under the wheels of the last two wagons of the train. The unfortunate woman sustained serious injuries, which necessitated both legs being amputated.
Anne Frusher said she had heard about this story from her father, he had witnessed the scene of the accident whilst on his way to Wisbech in Mr Welchmans car. She continued to tell me how her father picked Mrs Scott up, placed her in the car and sped off to the hospital at Wisbech.
Forty five year old Elizabeth Scott, incredibly survived the accident, she died in 1935 aged 66 having lived a further twenty one years.
Around 2008, this story came up in conversion with a lady in Brian Tweeds butcher shop. Jill Bliss, a relative to the Scotts told me they had only recently thrown away Mrs Scott's artificial legs that had been in her loft since she died.

Mr. William Welchman, pictured with his wife outside his House owned the first motorcar in Upwell. He bought his Daimler, registration number EB 1 at the turn of the 20th century.

We have mentioned the Hunter-Rowe family being benevolent towards Upwell and neighbouring villages. They were successful fruit growers as was another generous benefactor, Mr Albert Edward Morton.

There are many worthy projects that had a little help from this man. He would have been profoundly embarrassed if he was around to hear us mention them. His generosity towards a major village amenity has only recently been revealed. This, and much more was done anonymously at the time. Morton's orchards formed a major part of the "Spring Blossom Route" around the fenland villages that existed up to the 1970s. This was a local attraction that was "brown sign posted" and attracted visitors from all over the country.

The following tribute to Mr Morton was reported in the national magazine "The Grower" in 1957.

A remarkable crop of Cox on 50-year-old trees can be seen in the orchards of A., E. & R. G. Morton at Upwell, near Wisbech. Half a century ago Mr. A. E, Morton planted his first apple trees at Pingle Gardens. Since then the name of Morton has come to be respected wherever East Anglian growers get together.

From 1921 Mr. Morton won a prize at every imperial fruit show, until they finished. Among his awards were six gold medals, two silver and two bronze. At the Wisbech shows, the firm of A. E. & R. G., Morton (Mr. A. E. is now in partnership with his son) generally put in about 20 entries, most of which win some kind of award. The packers share the prize money.

Mr, Morion's grandfather was one of the first fruit-growers in the Wisbech area, and grew many of the older varieties of apple on his farm at Outwell. These included Dr. Harvey, Blenheim Orange, and what was thought to be Normanton Wonder. Mr. Morton's father was an arable farmer, but when A. E. made up his mind to emigrate to New Zealand,his grandfather stepped in to let him have a field at Upwell to start fruit growing so A. E. became a fruit-grower at the age of 25.

That was just 50 years ago. (1907)

Many of the original trees remain, and Cox on crab stock gives excellent crops (there were no selected stocks then to choose from, but the trees are little the worse for that).

Seven acres were planted up first, including Grenadier, Worcester, Early Victoria, Lane's Prince Albert, and a few Bramleys. In the 1914-18 war another 81 acres were added, and after the war came ten acres more.

Mr. Morton pointed out the Bramley trees, which had just had their fruit picked, "Look at the growth and quantity of those leaves," he said. "We reckon that it takes five leaves to make a blossom. And the buds are forming nicely. So I forecast another good crop of Bramleys next year—unless anything unforeseen happens."

Bit by bit the farm was built up, until now there are 33 acres of top fruit and four acres of soft. Altogether, with his son's holding, there are 98 acres to manage.

Mr Albert E Morton at the opening of St Andrews Chapel 1962

Serving the community seems to run in the family. Bernard Morton the son of A E Morton, and his wife has been involved with many village activities.

Bernard was not interested in fruit growing but preferred conventional farming like his grandfather George William Morton who started farming at Laddus Drove before moving to Upwell.

Bernard was chairman of Marshland Rural Council, and local JP.

He was chairman of the parish council, chairman of the playing field committee, chairman of Upwell County Primary school and drainage officer for Churchfield and Plawfield internal drainage board.

Bernard Morton and Walter Hunter-Rowe stood as guarantors during the time the playing field was purchased for the village. The playing field might have been sold to make way for a fuel station if the village had not bought it. Bernard was the parish council chairman when the village hall was bought by the council for £40,000 from Mr Foti.

A very contented Bernard Morton pictured at his Small Lode home in September 2012 aged 91.

He has contributed much time and energy to Upwell over many years and has been a faithful servant to the Methodist church.

A remarkable man, at the age of 80 he was still helping his cows to calf. Those who have done this will know how difficult the job can be.

LITTLEPORT RIOTS and LEE HOUSE

In 1815, the government increased taxation on imported wheat and grain to help pay for the costs of the Napoleonic Wars (1803–1815). Basic commodities, like cereals and bread, became heavily over-priced, creating widespread social unrest. The worst hit were the families of the men returning from the Battle of Waterloo who arrived home at a time when unemployment was already high. It was recorded to the Board of Agriculture in February, March, and April 1816 *"The state of the labouring poor is very deplorable, and arises entirely from the want of employment, which they are willing to seek, but the farmer cannot afford to furnish"*.

The ensuing unrest that began in Littleport and spread across the region was undoubtedly sparked by sheer desperation caused by starvation.

Families were made desperate for food which forced them to risk death, deportation and other harsh punishment.

The Reverend John Vachell tried to calm the rioters. Vachell had been vicar of St George's church Littleport since November 1795. He was a magistrate and a much disliked brutal, unpopular man. He tried to read the Riot Act without effect, the crowd told him to go home, and they would visit his house in good time which they duly did.

The 1,500 rioters, mainly men but some women besieged The Crown public house until the magistrates agreed to allow a deputation of eight rioters inside to make their pleas. Their request was to have work and be paid two-shillings per day. The magistrates agreed but they had already called the yeoman cavalry from Upwell.

Major William Lee, a gentlemen farmer, commanded a troop of the Norfolk Yeomanry Cavalry from his home in Upwell.

Major Lee attended the riots at Littleport, Downham Market and Wisbech. Taking his troops to Wisbech first, he quietened the rioters and then rode to Downham where the labourers held the sitting Magistrates as hostages. Ordering his troopers to use only the back of their swords, he secured a meeting, after which it was arranged that all should disperse, wages would be raised and that bygones should be bygones.

His tactful and humane action, so unlike the brutal conduct of so many local and military authorities at the time, was warmly welcomed by the Government. Major Lee received a letter of thanks from the Prince Regent with the offer of a Baronetcy. As he had no son, he declined this honour, however he was later appointed Deputy Lieutenant for Norfolk.

Lee House originally dates from mid 17th century but has been altered greatly. The "Whittlesea whites" brick regency frontage dates from around 1800 and likely to have been done by James Lee.

Towards the end of the 19th century the house had its own private gas supply, the Upwell and Outwell Gas Company could not guarantee a reliable supply. An acetylene gas plant was installed on the gable end wall in order to provide up-to-date lighting. The remains of the fixings can still be seen on the south-west facing wall. Acetylene gas was released by exposing calcium carbide into water.

Lee House has been the home of many doctors over the years including the renowned Dr Tubbs. Dr Paul Millard discovered there was at one time, a wool weaving business operated in one of the outbuildings.

Dr Tubbs at Lee House circa 1868.

The same wall plate supporting the gas lamp below the central window can still be seen today.

ICE SKATING AND CYCLING

When it comes to sport Upwell has to be rated extremely high amongst similar sized villages in England thanks to the Horn family. This family had two talented sons who were national champions and performed internationally in their sports, which were, ice speed skating and cycling. To do these two sportsmen justice one would have to write an entire book on their achievements, such was the measure of their success.

Cyril W. Horn was born in Upwell on the 7th October 1904. He lived almost opposite the old Salvation Army building near "The Crescent". He was one of six children and was the second eldest. Three of the boys were extremely dedicated sportsmen as indeed were their father and grandfather's family. Cyril would often recall the story when his Uncle Tom Sutton, an excellent skater, beat the famous Jim Smart at Littleport. His father was also a good skater but his trade as a blacksmith meant there was little time for practice. Cyril left school at the age of twelve to help his father tend five forges along with fourteen other workers. During the First World War (1914-18) they supplied horseshoes to the army, often working fourteen hours a day to fill the orders.

Walter Horn's Blacksmith shop at the Crescent circa 1914

Another enterprise taken on by Cyril's father was to be landlord of the White Lion Public House. Cyril was thirteen at the time and had to stand on a box to reach the pumps when serving the customers. As he was so young and small the customers called him "Baby Horn" which was later shortened to "Babs". This nickname stayed with him all his life.

Cyril Horn's interest in skating started when a customer came in the pub and gave him a pair of "fen runners". That afternoon there were some races held behind the blacksmith's shop almost opposite the pub. Cyril entered as a thirteen year old but could not skate so he ran round the track showing enough promise to cause interest in those watching. Two days later he was entered in a race at Outwell in the fourteen-year-old group. The races were organised by Mr. Bond the auctioneer. Cyril Horn's first competitive race was against Bert Bond, the auctioneer's son. Bond fell down during the race so it was started again and this time Cyril raced a lad called Smith as master Bond would not compete. The prize was 10 shillings and Cyril won. His next race was against Walter Ward who beat him, probably because Walter had the New Norwegian skates which were much superior to the old fen runners.

Skating:- C. W. Horn

Cyril was featured on cigarette cards published by Senior Service and Park Drive cigarettes in 1933 and 1935. It was No. 93 of 96 in the Senior Service set and No 34 of 48 in the park Drive set.

Description on one card:

The One Mile Speed Skating Race which followed (the exhibition skating) was contested by C.W. Horn, the Amateur Champion, D. Person, the Professional Champion, G.W. Martin and L. Stewart. Horn, skating beautifully, led from the start, and without ever being seriously extended, won in the excellent time of 3 min. 27 1-5 sec., which is the fastest time ever recorded for a mile on an enclosed rink.

Trivia: The 1924 winter games in Chamonix France. C W Horn was the youngest Participant: (19 years, 111 days)

Cyril (Babs) Horn was described on the back of the Senior Service cigarette card as: *"The fastest amateur skater in Great Britain and from 1927 to 1933 winner of the four British Championships held, his last triumph being in 1933 at Lingay Fen, Lincolnshire, with a time of 4.47¼ minutes over a 1½ mile course. The holding of these championships is entirely dependent on a very severe frost in order to freeze up this ideal skating course. In addition Horn holds the amateur records for 1½ mile 1929; 1 mile 1929 and 3 miles 1929, and a host of official skating trophies including International Amateur Race; Prince of Orange Bowl (1500 metre Circular Course); Duddleston Cup (1 mile race) - three successive wins including record time; Cameron Cup (¼ mile Race) twice; Warner Cup (1 mile race); and also held 1929 ¼ mile Championship of Great Britain."*

In 1924 and 1928 Cyril represented the UK at skating in the Winter Olympics. England has never been competitive in the winter sports and it was no different when Cyril was racing. The Scandinavians have access to much longer periods of cold weather. In the 1928 Olympics the 1500 metres was won with a time of 2 mins 21 secs. Cyril came 24th with a creditable time of 2 mins 40 secs.

Cyril was a national champion at both skating and cycling.

The ideal training was cycling so he and younger brother Dennis, who was also a good skater, took to cycling in the summer months. Cycling was another sport Cyril Horn excelled at, winning many national titles and in 1937 was overall English champion.

In a rare interview taped in 1980 when Cyril was 75 years of age he recalls how he was selected to represent Britain in the 1928 Olympics. The following is written exactly how Cyril Horn gave the interview.

"Many people have asked how I came to skate in the Olympics. Well, it was this way. Out on Welney Wash, a week before, my uncle, Bernie Sutton, skated against Fred Jackson of Welney and carrying my uncle's coat and trousers over my arm I skated round the outside of the course whilst them two was on the inside and I beat them both. My uncle won by about 30 yards. For a prize he got £2 and a leg of mutton, which he shared with my mother. On his return home to London he went to see

General Critchley, who was the head of the British skating team and told him that he had got a relation in the Fens that could beat anybody. That's the reason I got into the 1924 Olympics! They sent me out three days before the racing started, I'd never been on a oval track in my life, if they had put me on a fen river I'm certain that I could have beat them all, the ends beat me. The small turn was alright but the outer turn was about 105 yards round. I was inclined to skate hard and drift round the turn. Well, that's no good at all. I was watching this 'ere American skater on the T.V. the other night, he's got it right and I reckon he was the fittest man in the Olympics, well he should be with all the training they do with all them machines instead of being out on the land hoeing, digging and spreading manure like I did".

Cyril goes on to say how he was selected for the 1936 Olympics for cycling, he also states that his brother Dennis actually attended the event but the records do not support this. The facts were, they were the best in Britain at that time and should have been selected. There were many protests by various clubs but it was said, although the Horn brothers did well in England, they did not perform well abroad. It seems being an old fen boy did not carry favour with the selectors. Cyril challenged the man they sent in a 1000 metre time trial a few months after the Olympics and beat him at Herne Hill London by two seconds. Even more incredibly, Dennis Horn regularly recorded faster times than Cyril.

If these two local boys were taking part in sport today, the modern media coverage would make Upwell the centre of national cycle racing.

D. S. HORN
ENGLISH CHAMPION 1930-1931-1932-1933-1934
WINNER OF LEON MEREDITH 1931-1932-1933-1934

In the decade 1930 to 1940 Dennis Horn was the greatest sprint cyclist in the UK being almost unbeatable in the 25-mile sprint event. His vast collections of trophies included the much sought after Muratti Gold Cup. Early on in his career Dennis won the trophy outright after wins in 1931-32 and 33. He lost it to the German sprinter Toni Merkens in 1934, and then went on to win the replacement trophy for the next two years.

The Horn brothers were sponsored by Claude Butler who made one of the best racing cycles money could buy at the time. One international advertisement read: *Claude Butler provides bikes to international racers such as Reg Harris, Eileen Sheridan, Peter Underwood and Dennis Sutton Horn.* Claude Butler bikes were ridden at the 1931 world championship in Copenhagen and then in Italy (1932), France (1933), Germany (1934). They were also used at the Los Angeles Olympics in 1932.

Dennis Sutton Horn is seen displaying a few of his impressive collection of trophies. He is pictured sitting on his Claude Butler cycle that is on loan and displayed at the March cycle museum.

As has previously been said, to do these two sportsmen justice we could fill a sizeable book, such were their achievements.

There have been a few other very good skaters and cyclists in Upwell over the years who had been inspired by the Horns. Frank Rayner was known to be a very strong skater and he won the prestigious three miles Hayes Fisher Cup which was at the time a professional event.

Peter Dorling was another excellent skater winning all the professional trophies in late 1960s and mid 1970s, but Peter's great love was cycling. When Peter rode 25 miles in under the hour, a mature "Babs" Horn told him he could now call himself a cyclist! That was a genuine very well received compliment from a great athlete.

Lilian Ream

Peter Dorling was the British professional speed skating champion in 1969.
He is pictured after winning the Hayes Fisher cup at Swavesey.

Peter came to the sport quite late in life he was inspired by an Outwell legend the late Jack Cousins.
Jack Cousins encouraged many youngsters to take up sport and is one of the area's unsung heroes.

Peter Dorling on his hand built road bike circa 1980.

Peter, a farmer from Stratford House, Back Drove, Upwell was a keen veteran member of the Wisbech Wheelers and became a multiple record holder.

He was awarded a very rare certificate of achievement from the Veterans Time Trail association.

It was common for Peter to get up at 0400 hrs and ride to Littleport and home before breakfast during his demanding training sessions.

In 1980, at the age of 43 he rode a solo 10 mile, in 21mins 24 secs, the fastest time in the country by a veteran at that time. Also in 1980 he did a 50 mile ride in 2hrs 4 mins.

He won the Wisbech Wheelers open 25 mile time trial in a time of 56 mins 51 secs at the age of 44, which was the course and event record at the time. These performances could only be reached by an extremely dedicated sportsman.

FOOTBALL

Some Upwell men decided to seek out information regarding the history of Upwell Town Football Club. I encountered two of them one day in the Wisbech library sweating over the old newspaper clippings contained within the microfiche. As an old hand at research I had a chat with them during one of my many trips to the reference section in the library. I suspected they did not know what they had let themselves in for as there is a mountain of information kept at the library and the Wisbech Museum.

These two gentlemen soon discovered the task they were facing was immense. Through dogged determination and sheer hard work over a long period of time they finally completed the history of the Upwell Town football Club. They have produced a superb document, detailing the club's fortunes over the past 108 years. I am deeply indebted to Mr. Geoffrey Barrett, John Francis and their friends for allowing me to include some of their work in this book.

The first recorded details of Upwell Town Football Club were found in the Wisbech Advertiser supplement 15 April 1894. It was a game against Wisbech Cassandra and the score was 3-3. The next year (20 November 1895) the club was properly formed with the following appearing in Wisbech Standard.

For some time past a desire has been strongly felt by the lovers of the game to form a Football Club in Upwell and in pursuance of the public notice issued by Mr H. J. Webber and the Rev. W.C. Thompson of Upwell, to consider the advisability of forming a club, a meeting was convened at the " Five Bells Inn" on Wednesday last.

The following were present: Rev. W.C. Thompson, Dr. Jameson, Messrs. J Webber, F. W. Newell, F. Ely, T. Shepherd, T. Jakens, J. W. Vurley, H. Dales, C. H. Hythe, C. Overland Jr and others. The Rev. W. C. Thompson was voted the Chairman. After explaining the object of the meeting the chairman called upon Mr. H.J. Webber to inform the meeting what was proposed to be done in the formation of the club. He explained that the game was "exceedingly" popular and as a player of several years standing he assured them that it was a means of enjoyment, even if at times their shins suffered. He hoped they would be able to command a good set of members, which meant a good club. He then proposed that the football club would be formed, Dr. Jameson seconded and it was carried unanimously. Mr Newell proposed that the club use the rules of the English association, which was carried. Mr H. J. Webber said he had much pleasure in proposing the name of Mr. Welchman as club president, Dr. Jameson supported the proposal. Mr. J. E. Hartley allowed his field near the Public Hall to be used free of charge, this field is still used today by the village football club.

Mr. H. J. Webber was the first captain of the club and the following were amongst the first to play: W. Inman, Rev. Thompson, H. J. Webber, C. Blythe, Dr. Jameson, T. Rallison, S. Ellis, H. Jakens, Meagre, P. Handley, S. Ellis, J. Townley, Foster, Coates, Carver, Newling.

The first ever encounter with the emerging enemy Outwell, took place on Mr. Hartley's field near the Public Hall 23rd April 1897 and Upwell came out 3-1 winners. Later Outwell was to re-join Upwell for important games against the nearby towns of Wisbech and March. For a short while in the beginning, the two villages shared the same facilities, in fact there was one just team. At one time Upwell Town football Club was in the same league as Wisbech and other similar sized towns and produced some very good teams. In 1907 the list of registered players included C. W. H. Whalley, Walter Horn, James Booty, Albert Tombleson, Charles Bettison, John Barrett, Charles Parker, Bernard Sutton, George Francis, William Carrie, Leonard Young,

Circa 1920

Hugh Francis, William Johnson, Alex King, Henry Sutton, Robert Tomlinson, Walter Bains, George Shepperson, William Gray, George Smith, John Edward Francis, George Mitcham, Ernest Prudin, Isaac Smith, Henry and Alfred Sayer.

All clubs and organisations have the unsung heroes without which they could not operate. The founder members of the football club have been mentioned but over the years there have been many people who have given their money and time to ensure the village football team has survived to the present day. It is only right some of these people are mentioned and get the credit they deserve.

1908-9 Mr. A. Allott, I. Smith, A. King, C. Parker, Mr. H. Gardener, Mr. G. Smith.

1926-27. T. W. Hill, Mr. Brundish, Mr. J. Wilson, Mr. Lance Hunter-Rowe, Mr. W. Horn, B. Webber, G. Webster, G. Smith, E. Johnson, H. Judd, I. Youngs, C. Parker 1928–29. T. W. Hill, Mr. A. Brundish, E. Johnson, G. Smith, J. Wilson, Committee: B. Webber, G. A. Smith, L. Hunter-Rowe, W. Johnson, J. Stittle, H. Horn, E. Vurley, A. Lee, B. Overland, H. Overland, S. Larmeth, R. Dorman, R. Britchford, B. Johnson, Rev. S. Baker.

The 1924-25 team and club members

At the annual general meeting of 1934-35 in the parish rooms it was announced the following would be in charge for the next season. President Miss D. Hill, Secretary Mr. Mayhew, Chairman Mr Webber, Vice Chairmen Mr E. Johnson, Treasurer Mr. E. Johnson and Mr. W. Reedman. Committee: O. Agger, C. Wallace, J. Parker, W. Allen, W. Horn, E. Young, D. Garner, E. Judd, E. Woodman, A. Carver, J. W. Young. The grounds-man was Mr Stocks.

A letter of thanks was sent to Mr. Overland of the White Lion for the use of the changing room.

There was an article published in the local paper 26th August 1938 acknowledging the club being one of the first football clubs in the area and lists the players taking part in the first match.

The article also mentions Mr. T.W. Hill purchasing the sports field so that games could be played.

Upwell Town F.C. 1947

Standing at the rear left:

Mr. Lance Hunter-Rowe, Mike Francis, Sam Reedman, Derek Lunn.
middle row: Tich Longmuir, G. Rumblo, M. Webb.
front row: Peter Dorman, R. Rumblo, Jess Lister, Hugh Beckett and Norman Wenn. The young man leaning on the goalpost is John Francis aged seven.

My father in law Reg Smith, a keen Outwell player, often mentioned the lively games he had against Upwell. The records show Outwell beat Upwell 4 –3 just before the start of the Second World War and my father in law was in the Outwell team at that time. Shortly after that game he was called up for duty in the war. The match was on the 3rd of November 1939. For Upwell the team was Dorman, Welfare, Godfrey, M. Francis, Reedman, E. Francis, Lunn, Sutton, Beckett, Watson and Wenn.

Outwell: Green, Betty, Reg Smith, Ron Smith, Wilson, D. Cousins, J. Cousins, B. Sutton, Longmuir, F. Sutton, and W. Ward.

At the annual general meeting 22nd July 1949 Upwell decided to join the Peterborough League Division 1. The reserves joined the Lynn League.

President C. W. Brighty, Chairman B. Webber, Secretary W. E. Reedman, Treasurer F. E. Johnson. Committee: O. Agger, R. Lister, D. Lunn, C. Wallis, J. Stittle, R. Smith, B. Brooks and H. J. Wright.

Upwell 1948-49

Standing L/R: Les Young, Ross Lister, Jack Stittle, Bert Brooks, Owen Agger, Cecil Grey, Ernie Johnson, Cecil Wallis, Lance Hunter-Rowe, Walter Reedman, Ben Webber. M/r. Harold Wright, W. Dorman, Tich Longmuir, Derek Risebrow, Willy Roessler, Jess Lister, Bernie Morton, D. Lunn. F/r. Graham Hood? Peter Dorman, Peter Stittle, Jack Plumb, Graham Stittle and Norman Wenn.

Local football was entering into a period that might be described as the most popular period. Home games were well-attended pre-war, it was common to see over 200 people at local football matches.

Both Upwell and Outwell had large wooden grandstands built just before the war. In the 1940s supporters were able to travel on the specially hired buses to away games. Spectators were expected to pay at the gate to see players such as Roessler, Hempson, Lunn, Garner, Lister, Longmuir, Risebrow, Stittle, Frost, Laboda and Plumb beat a team called Blackstones 5-1 in 1949.

The A.G. M. 19th June 1953.

Leading goal scorers: R. Frost 36, J. Plumb 12, P. Stittle 11 and D. Risebrow 9.

Chairman B. Webber, V-Chairman B. Morton, Secretary D. Lunn, Ass. Secretary W. Reedman, Treasurer E. Johnson. Committee: O. Agger, R. Smith, A. Quince, C. Wallis, G. Stittle, H. Beckett, L. Secker, E. Hardy, D. Overland and R. Poole.

A. G. M. 8th June 1962

President B. Morton, Chairman E. Johnson, V-Chairman M. Roberts, Secretary A.R. Clingo and B. Webber, Treasurer M. Owens.

A.G.M. 30th June 1967.

Mr. F.E. Johnson resigned his position as club chairman due to poor health. He was made a life member and thanked for his considerable contributions to the club for over 40 years.

President: B.E. Morton, V- Presidents Mr. L. H. Rowe, E. F. Hancock, Ross Lister, F. Day, C. W. Brighty and R. Hunter. Life Vice President Mr. B. Webber. Life Members were: O. Agger, W. E. Reedman.

Chairman B. Matthews. Vice Chairman R. Titmarsh, Secretary P. E. Johnson. Treasurer Mr. A. Lunn. Team Secretary Mr. A. Hall. Fixture Secretary J. Wake. Committee: Mr. T. Lunn, G. Barrett, G. Matthews, P. Moden, B. Crockford, D. Pope, H. Hall, R. Forth, J. Goodman, J. Welch, E.W. Lawrence and E. Mackrill. Playing Field Rep Mr. D. Pope.

A. G. M. 26th June 1972 President E. Johnson, Chairman: R. Boyce. V-Chairman J. Plumb. Secretary G. Barrett. Treasurer A. Lunn. Fixture Secretary J. Goodman.

A.G. M. 22nd June 1973.

President F.E. Johnson, Vice Presidents D. Gooch, W. Means, L. H. Rowe, D. Hircock, W. J. Brighty, J. Vaughn, E. Tweed, B. Morton, M. Owens, S. Jarvis, E. Hancock, H. Crane and E. Macrill.
Chairmen were R. Boyce and V. C. B. Boyce. Secretaries: G. Barrett and V. Goodman. Treasurer R. Lunn. Committee: C. Lunn, M. Lunn, A. Clingo, F. Follen, B. Horn, S. Mills, P. Moden, R. Lunn, G. Youngs and A. Pope. Grounds-man was Mr. C. Judd.

On the 27th of December 1973 a bombshell hit the Village as the football club announced its withdrawal from the Peterborough league but the reserve team continued to play in the Kings Lynn League.
On The 13th of September 1974 Old Lenns beat Upwell Town football team on their return to the Lynn League first division.
Today it seems village football is in decline having been a popular pastime for more than a hundred years. There are other sports and hobbies available to the modern youth, many of which require money and travel, both of which seems, more readily available today.
Village football was a community building exercise that was supported by all. It was an "occasion", it entertained us both watching and playing. It was an honour to be selected to play for your village and there was passion, especially when the opponents were the neighbouring village. The teams were selected from the locals. It was quite rare for a player to be from a neighbouring village. Perhaps this is why the games with the next village were so lively.
The local football teams have much better facilities now with centrally heated changing rooms and nice hot showers waiting for them after a game.
Gone are the days when players had to clear the cattle off the pitch, dig the ball out of cowpats and put their kit on in adverse conditions. The balls are lighter, the grass is shorter, the shirts and boots are generally the right size. There are no more "American Westerns Comic Books" for shin pads and leather boots weighing a ton when the mud stuck between the "layered leather" studs. Perhaps one day local football will once again be the highlight of the week for village folk but somehow I doubt it. We have to greatly admire those who organise the modern game and persevere with keeping local football alive today.

Upwell Town FC. 1957-58.

Back row: Peter Dorman, Russell Melton, Michael Lunn, John Francis, Bob Roseberry and Derek Walker. Front row: John Steer, John Barr, David Bennett, Alan Woolner and Brian Boyce.

Football club annual dinner at the White Lion circa 1949

MOTOR CYCLE RACING

Hugh Warrington Brown, the son of an Upwell smallholder always had an intense interest in motorbikes much to the displeasure of his family. His parents' profound aversion to motorbikes was probably caused by a tragic fatal accident involving the son of their next-door neighbour Jack Webb on the Basin Corner Outwell in the early 1930s.

Hugh was born in a cottage near the old Wesleyan Chapel on the 20th November 1916. His great grandfather was landlord of the White Lion public house for 47 years, Walter Horn succeeded him. It was during this time another well-known Upwell man and family friend, Wilby Jarvis, was taken prisoner in the First World War.

Hugh had a great uncle with an interesting name. He was called John Beaupré Bell Clee. It was not clear how this chap acquired his middle name but it is thought the family was not related to the well-known Beauprés of Beaupré Hall.

Hugh's father Charles bought Piermont House in 1918 for £260, where Hugh spent all his childhood and it is still the family house today. Charles William Brown left school at 13 and worked for Spikings the butchers whose shop was next door to the White Lion, where he was brought up. At the age of 13 he was paid one shilling and sixpence a week. Brian Tweed is the present day owner of this shop. Hugh attended what is now called Upwell County Primary School until the age of 14. On leaving school he started working life with his father and brother Bernard, on their smallholding.

Hugh acquired his riding skills at an early age by racing around the fields near his home on old motorbikes "faked" up by his brother Bernard. His first road machine was a 350cc Velocette, which he purchased for £12 in 1933 at the age of 16.

He bought a brand new Norton model 18 in 1934 from W. H. Rose of March for £65.00.

Mr Rose was a well-known national sidecar champion in his younger days. There was a succession of Nortons after that including international models.

In September 1945 Hugh and two friends, Joe Carter and Richard (speedy) Bettinson, set off for Stourbridge West Midlands on the outskirts of Birmingham, to purchase his pride and joy the famous 1939 490cc overhead cam Manx Norton capable of 110 m.p.h.

I can hear the Japanese fanatics of today saying "110 m.p.h. that's a bit pedestrian".

Could I suggest they have a go on a 1940s British bike and find the courage and take it up to 80 m.p.h. It is about that speed when the tyres and your backside go elliptical, the vibration starts to impede your vision and your muscles are on fire. I wonder how many have further courage to then proceed to the maximum speed. It can be seen later, not many, judging by the number of owners this old bike had after Hugh Brown sold it. Modern motorbikes cannot normally produce this "precarious" experience at any speed.

Hugh Brown on the 1939 490cc overhead cam Manx Norton

Hugh later raced this machine at the top venues such as Cadwell Park and Snetterton and rubbed shoulders with the very best at that time. Racing in those days was much the same as it is today, finances dictated how competitive one could be.

To be successful one has to have the resources to obtain the best equipment and support. Hugh simply could not compete with the likes of John Surtees and Bob McIntyre on account of their superior machinery but he certainly gave Frank Sheene a run for his money. Frank Sheene's son Barry, as we all know, did make the top flight. There is little doubt, if Hugh Brown had had the funds he would have been right there with the very best as he turned in good performances with equipment 15 years out of date. It is difficult to find out just how well Hugh did, as he is an extremely modest man and quick to praise others. One thing is certain, he could ride a motorcycle better than most as he proved in over 40 years of, in his words, a very enjoyable pastime. Dennis Ward of Wisbech rebuilt the old bike in 1951. The 1939 engine and gearbox were fitted to the very latest Norton Feather Bed frame, which later became part of the legendary Trident along with the BSA front forks and the Triumph engine.

Hugh Brown's 1950s Norton

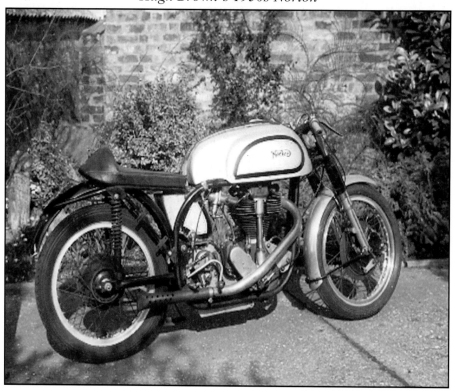

Hugh Brown stopped riding in 1973 and he lovingly looked after his old Norton in its retirement for the next 20 odd years at his home in Upwell. Mr. Ronald Shilvock of Wolferton near Kings Lynn bought the bike in about 1994 and it was then re-sold to Graham Osborne of North Walsham. Mr. Andrew Heanes of Clacton paid something like £6,800 for the bike in 1997 then on to Mr. Barry Stickland who was the chairman of the British Norton members club.

When speaking to Mr. Stickland about the bike's recent history, I mentioned how surprised I was to see how many owners the old Norton had had since Hugh Brown sold it.

It seems the Japanese bike fans found the old 1952-updated version of the Norton a beast to ride and difficult to handle. Whatever would they have thought of the original 1939 machine? That has to be a superb testament to Hugh Warrington Brown's riding skills.

Showing another version of the 1936 Norton racing at Cadwell

When I was young and just getting into motorbikes I remember watching Hugh Brown turn heads as he rode through the village on his Manx Norton. One regular trip he used to make was to zip off to Hunstanton and back on a Sunday morning before breakfast. Another little story that has remained in my memory is my first trip to Snetterton.

I had just bought my first road motorcycle so my friend Ted Simmons and I decided to go to Snetterton to see the motorcycle racing. My bike was a 10 year old 200cc Arial Colt, Ted had an all singing all dancing brand new Italian 175cc Parilla racing machine.

In those days it was unusual for me to go to Wisbech never mind some far away place like Snetterton. Most of our friends were of the opinion that I would not get as far as Downham Market. We set off one bright Saturday morning nice and steady.

Ted was the navigator with me trailing behind. Somehow we missed a road sign and were heading towards Newmarket. We called into a garage to check our bearings where a nice chap thought it was humorous to send us in the wrong direction. We had a clue something was wrong when we noticed all the flash motorbikes going in the opposite direction to us.

Eventually we arrived at the racetrack. Just as we were about to enter the main gate Ted's bike stalled and simply would not start. Some well informed motorcycle enthusiasts tried to help but the new electronics were beyond them.

We watched the racing not thinking much about how we were going to solve our problem. There were not many mobile phones about in 1963 so it was decided I would inform Ted's father on my arrival home in the hope he could recover Ted and his machine. On leaving the racetrack I suddenly realised another problem, I did not know the way home. Just then I had a stroke of luck. A familiar sight cruised by me on the road to Thetford. I thought great that's Mr. Brown he will be going home to Upwell I'll follow him. He rode at a steady speed until we reached the Thetford Straight.

He then opened up his machine and quickly disappeared. From that point on I knew the way home and I followed the smell of the Castrol "R30" enriched exhaust fumes from Hugh Brown's Norton.

FIVE BELLS ANGLING CLUB

The Five Bells fishing club was formed circa 1950 and boasted over sixty members at its peak. The landlord of the Five Bells was Mr. M. Owen at this time. Records show Mr. J. Parker was chairman in 1952. Mr R. Parker was voted chairman in 1957 after being proposed by Neville Curtis and seconded by Edward Canham. During that meeting the following were also appointed. Mr. George Clare of Wisbech proposed and William Lilly seconded, Neville Curtis as vice chairman. Mr. Clare was the proprietor of a fishing tackle shop on the junction of Union Street and Hill Street Wisbech and was a member of the club for many Years. Other members of the club holding various positions in the early days were: H. Hines, A. Whitrod, R. Goult, B. Bonnet, R. Gooch, S. Bradley, S. Cragg, G. Bowles, S. Tegerdine, C. Butcher, P. Archer, J. Watson, R. Jackson, G. Archer, L. Peacock, R. Holmes, R. Duff, F. Dunham, T. Booty, B. Booty, P. Hammond, R. Peachy, J. Norman, L. Duncan, L. Millingan, Mr Eke, N. Cousins.

Some members of the Olde Mill Angling club

Mr. N. Curtis became chairman in 1959 and was made a life member in 1970, later he became president in 1971 succeeding Mr Norman Cousins. During a meeting in 1971 it was proposed ladies could be members of the club and take part in matches but this was deferred for the annual general meeting later that year. As the A.G.M progressed a further proposal was expected but was not made, much to the discord of many. The records do not mention lady anglers until the early 1980s when girls could compete against the boys. In 1987 The Olde Mill Upwell invited the club to use their facilities with the promises of sponsorship from the Breweries. The club changed its name to the Olde Mill Angling Club shortly after that invitation.

During the clubs very successful 44-year history they were responsible for much enjoyment besides angling matches. Tickets for their annual dinner and dance at Three Holes Public Hall were highly popular and usually sell outs with entertainment often being supplied by Sounds Familiar. In the early days Oliver Barrowclough played records from his enormous collection. I suppose "Ollie" was one of the first D.Js. in the area although discotheques and disc jockeys were unheard of then. There was one occasion when events did not go to plan as reported in the minutes book on the 11th of April 1969. The chairman, Mr. Neville Curtis reported that "this was the worst dinner he had attended" as it was too cold and the entertainment fell short of expectations. Tombola was another popular pastime at Outwell village hall with Ted Canham usually being the caller. Ted Canham was the local water bailiff for many years and had the arduous task of putting the stakes or pegs in for the hundreds of anglers from the Sheffield area for their weekend fishing. The local water was taken over by the Yorkshire clubs at the weekends making angling difficult for the locals. I know the chaps from the pits did not take kindly to us young boys having a swim down the Pingle on a hot summer's day during their match. Tragically, one chap decided to join us one afternoon after a match in about 1962. He dived in from the bridge and did not surface for what seemed like hours. Several of his colleagues dived down in an effort to locate him without success. His body later emerged quite some way from the bridge.

Another tragedy occurred in 1974. Ian Rex Curtis followed his father to become a committee member and was a keen angler from an early age. As a young boy Ian lived at number 1 Glenfield Close Outwell. He would often go fishing with his friends, Roger Dack, the Trundle boys, Peter Howard, John Murkin, David Good and me. On the morning of Saturday 14th of September 1974 Ian set off with Ted Canham the water bailiff, to install the pegs for the next day's fishing on the banks of the middle level main drain near Neeps Bridge. About a half-mile away some young boys were shooting pigeons with a .22 rifle. Unfortunately Ian was accidentally hit with a single shot and sadly died from his injuries; he was just 26 years of age. It saddens me greatly to record this story as he was a good childhood friend and an extremely nice guy to know. By recording this small tribute to him ensures that all who were fortunate enough to know Ian remember him with fondness and respect. Most of us lads liked to talk to the Yorkshire fishermen on the weekends and go hunting for floats, soft drink bottles (we could get 3d for the empties from the Corona depot) and bits of kit left by the fishermen. It was interesting for us young boys from the country to listen to stories about coal mining and work in the steel industries. Some of these chaps had little black spots on their faces and hands. I remember learning about "face workers" and "blasters". One story I have told apprentices many times is of a company called Steads. Steads were famous throughout the world for making high quality engineering tools amongst other things. They were based in Sheffield, the epicentre of the world in terms of products manufactured in steel at one time. About 1932, Steads received a package from an engineering company in America. When the package was opened they found a "hardened steel drill bit" no larger in diameter than a human hair.

A message that accompanied the package said "beat this"! The Americans were so proud of their seemingly superior engineering skills they sought to embarrass one of the leading tool manufacturers of the world. Their drill bit was indeed small by most standards. One week after receiving the package Steads sent the drill bit back to America with the message, "you might catch up one day". The Americans examined their tiny drill bit and found Steads had drilled a hole down the middle.

It is interesting to peruse the records of the fishing matches over the years. It seemed to me as a boy that anglers filled their nets on a good day but the records reveal a different story. I found it surprising that so many matches were won with less than 10 pounds of fish!

The following are just a few results from the record books. Challenge shield 1956 J. R. Parker, 8lbs 15 oz. Club match at the aqueduct 1958 R. Duff, 5lbs 6½ oz. (both matches over 3 hrs) Challenge match 1958 (2hrs) J. R. Parker, 16lbs 1½ oz Morton's Bridge. Five Bells challenge cup (5hrs) R. Duff, 23lb 7 oz from the aqueduct to Pingle Bridge. Club match 1959 E. Canham (3hrs) 3lbs 8½ oz. In 1960 F. Duff won the Pewter Cup with 7lb 10 oz, the Rolfe Cup was won by F. Whitwell with 5lb 4 oz, Challenge Shield won by E. Canham with 8lb 8 oz. In 1961, N. Curtis won the landlord's cup with 3lb 12½ oz. In the next 5 years there were 15 matches with the highest catch being just 10 lb 3 oz. In 1964 F. Watson won the Winter Cup with just 1lb 8½ oz. The most fish caught ever recorded by the club was in 1966 when J. R. Parker won the Challenge Cup with 23lbs 5 oz during a five hour match. This must have been a good day with the rod as the first eight competitors notched up more than 10 lbs. There is nothing in the records to tell us of match results after 1966.

Showing off the spoils in the late 1960s

At the 44th Annual General Meeting at the Olde Mill the chairman Mr. P. Archer spoke of his disappointment at the lack of support the club had received the previous year. At this meeting it was agreed by all the members present that the club would suspend events for twelve months. This indicated the club would hold no matches and enter into no team events for the 1994 season. The last meeting was held at the Olde Mill on Sunday 30th of April 1995, those present were Peter Archer, Chairman. Edward (Ted) Canham, Treasurer. R. Archer, Secretary. J. Allen, P. Allen, D. Barnard, J. Pearce, M. Sindle, committee members. All records relating to the Five Bells Angling Club are now in the Wisbech and Fenland Museum. They will be preserved for future generations to study some village social history.

Footnote:

In Loving Memory
of

Ian Rex Curtis

Beloved son of Eileen and Neville

who died tragically on Saturday, 14th September, 1974

Aged 26 years

—

Service at St. Clement's Church, Outwell on
Friday, 20th September, 1974 at 9.30 a.m.

Followed by Cremation at Peterborough at 11 a.m.

Donations if desired may be left at the Church
in aid of Dr. Barnardo's Homes

" Berville "
Church Drove, Outwell

The day Ian Curtis died I was working on my house. Late in the evening PC Poole, the local policeman, called to see me.

I frequently worked late into the night in those days and Mr Poole often called round for a chat and a brew.

On this occasion he was extremely upset, for a time he did not speak.

After a while he told me the devastating news.

Mr Poole was aware we grew up together and were good friends. This was a sad loss to the community and to everyone that knew Ian Curtis.

It is often said, "God calls the best first"; well he certainly did on this occasion. Young men do not come along much better.

OTHER SPORTS

There was a thriving equestrian centre on the Outwell Upwell border that sadly only lasted about 20 years. Mill Lodge Equestrian Centre opened in the early 1970s and was fronted by a grand manor style house that was built (1974) and run by Mr. David Edgson.

The venue attracted the very top riders from national and international teams. The centre put on some important events including junior internationals. In 1981 they staged a junior international event, which they won with the leading team member James Edgson, son of the owner, winning three events. The site is now called Millers Rest.

The village playing field was used for all manner of activities over the years including equestrian events.

BOWLS

Upwell has a well attended outdoor bowls club that has existed over 70 years. Research into the club's history is ongoing and will appear in a future a publication.

CRICKET

Similarly to bowls, research into the history of Upwell cricket club will be published in a future book.

TENNIS

Upwell had a popular tennis club starting from the 1930s. The full history of the club is to follow in a future publication.

Includes: Kath Naylor, Madeline Floyd, Nora Russell, George Frusher, Richard Bowers, Harold Means, Ernest Hancock, Madge Cox, Bert Blackshore.

Includes: Mary Boyce, Geoff Rumblo, Madge Steer, Mary Furness, John Harnwell, Ernie Hancock, Tom Thomas.

ST. PETER'S CHURCH

There have been many documents published recording the history of St. Peter's Church. Dr. A. H. V. de Montgomery wrote perhaps the most detailed description in 1940. I will not attempt to improve his account nor that of many others but feel I should include some mention of Upwell St. Peter's Church within this book.

I have found some interesting pictures and historical details not widely published. During the course of research over many years, it was seen that the ancient parentage of the church is well recorded so I have only touched on that section. I believe it is important to be aware of how our churches are named and to have some knowledge of those our churches are dedicated to.

It seems "Peter" should really be Simon, who came from a small village called Bethesaida in Galilee. He and his family were fishermen, which brought him in contact with Jesus who took him to be one of his disciples. Jesus gave Simon a new name "Cephas" which translates into English as Peter. Peter was in one of the most trusted inner groups and shared the important experiences of Jesus. After the resurrection Peter carried on teaching in Jerusalem and other Mediterranean lands even though he experienced much persecution.

It appears Saint Peter died in Rome under Nero in the first century. Nero succeeded his stepfather Claudius in 54 A.D. and was famed for cruelty and corruption. He was blamed for the great fire of Rome in 64 A.D. during the persecution of the Christians.

THE EMPEROR NERO (A.D. 37-68)

There are some leaflets available in the church, also for the more serious student a detailed account can be found in the "Victoria History of Cambridgeshire" available at the Wisbech Library.

For many people, reading about the history of a church can be a little daunting and I must admit the manner in which church and ecclesiastical history is recorded can be frustrating. Books of this kind tend to be written by academics that are trained to use the English language as it should be used. The only issue with that is, sometimes we do not entirely appreciate quite what has been written. I will freely admit to being one of those people and I know many more like minded folk who would not admit to it.

Probably the earliest existing image of St Peter's church facing Church Lane.
Circa 1817

The tower supported a high wooden spire that was removed in 1842.

The original engraved lithograph is taken from a drawing by J.S. Cotman of Norwich.

I have attempted to record some of the history of St. Peter's Church in a way that is interesting and enjoyable and hope you will persevere when reading about one of our finest rural churches.

Upwell Church is dedicated to Saint Peter and Saint Paul, initially a 13th century church but, as can be seen later, very little 13th century work remains. It is the oldest and most important structure in the village and it has evolved much the same as many other fenland churches. Over the centuries, alterations have been made and extensions been added to arrive at the magnificent building we see today. William Watson, author of the History of Wisbech published in 1827, described the church as "a handsome pile of building". The church is located near the site of the original market place granted by King John, which at that time was the hub of the community and gave Welle or Wella its town status. Following an interesting conversation one Saturday morning in the Wisbech Museum with an eminent visitor from the Cambridge archaeological finds department, I discovered, when the Saxons spoke they often ended a word with "er". So, "Wella" actually could be "Well"; this to me sounds more logical, as a "Well" is where you would find water, which was abundant in this area for centuries.

There was an earlier religious house founded by St. Ethelreda in the 7th century on the site of what is now called "Welle Manor" and possibly a Norman church on Saxon foundations around the west wing area *(The history of the old vicarage will be covered later in the book)*.

The building materials used on St. Peters Church are brick, rag and Barnack stone with a small modern section blocking off the 15th century porch from the 14th century side entrance. These materials would have undoubtedly been transported to the site by boat using the Well(e) Stream, which carried the waters of the Wissey, Lark, Ouse (West Water) and medieval Nene. The Wellstream story will be covered later but, for now, it is important to know this old waterway was arguably the most important river in the Fens. It passed the site of Upwell Church centuries before the church was built and encouraged settlements.

The earliest parts of the present building are the west wall of the nave (facing the Five Bells public house) and the lower sections of the tower, which are of the early part of the 13th century. The oldest recorded relic found is on a stone cross, dedicated to Walter Le Curtis who lived in

Upwell and fought in the crusades in 1220. The History of Norfolk by The Rev. Francis Bloomfield published in 1770 mentions, *"on the floor lays a stone in the shape of a coffin and adorned with a tablet bearing a cross" (Blomefield described the cross as being "Pateé").* Seen on the coat of arms is the "Municipalité de la Paroisse de Saint-Philemon", *this appears to relate to St. Paul !* This normally signifies a crusader's coffin and dates from Saxon times. The records of the Abbey of Ramsey kept in the British Museum London mention Walter le Curtis as being the Custodian and Chief Man of the town of Welle as drawn up in the first year of King John, 1199.

This stone commemorating Walter le Curtis is now embedded in the south wall of the church facing the rectory.

The east arch of the tower is relatively modern which suggests there may have been a north aisle to the nave at one time. An eight-sided section was built to the tower in the 14th century and this forms the third stage. The base of the tower has arches on the south side (15th century) and east side (13th century) that are now blocked.

The bell tower was subject to extensive rebuilding in the mid 15th century. John Bayker, who was curate of St. Mary's Church, Welney, left 3s 4d to the tower in 1440. The following people also made contributions: Thomas Breste 1452, Kath Dowdenott 1456, K. Lawys 1459, Alice Thowry 1559, Robert Craneforth 1468, William Frost 1471, John Lawys 1474, John Bunthorn 1492, Richard Mann 1495, William Wrynche, John Machon and Peter Wolle 1499, William Shortwood 1509, John Harris 1517, John Everard 1521 and Roger Wan. The tower was finished in the 15th century but the bells were still being added up to 1539. In 1552 King Edward VI ordered his commissioners to confiscate 4 bells leaving only the Sanctus bell (Latin for sacred).

There are six bells dating from the 17th century onwards. The tenor bell weighing over 14 CWT (654Kg) measures 44 inches across (1.1m diameter) and it hangs within an iron frame in the belfry. They are inscribed as follows: John Draper made me 1613. John Draper made me 1627. Thomas Norris made me 1634. Robert Johnson, Robert Failes, Charles War, Joseph Mallows of East Dereham made the others in 1760. The bells were refurbished by C. & G. Mears, Founders, London, in 1856 under the instruction of the Rector Rev. W. Gale Townley. The churchwardens at this time were Robert Seayears and Joseph Bennington.

The bells lay silent in 1992 with no available funds to have them repaired. Local man, Mr Graham Tidmas, following his retirement, volunteered to help repair them free of charge. After the bells were placed to one side in the tower, the monumental task of removing the head-stocks and bringing them down for repair was engineered by Mr Tidmas. This was a task he was not familiar with. After all the head-stock bearings had been replaced, Mr (Bluey) Tidmas reinstated the bells. He remarked to the Rev. Thomas Heggs "I suppose I might live to regret fixing your bells considering I am retired and I live opposite the church"!

*The church
underwent extensive
restoration in the mid
19th century which
included the
installation of the
galleries and the
pews in the aisle.*

*The aisle pews were
permanently removed
in the 1950s.
They can be seen
today in the Five
Bells Public House.*

Great effort was made in the 16th century to remove all reference to Rome. On the south side near the pulpit is a stone spiral staircase leading up to the roof and to where the Sanctus bell was situated. When viewed from New Road, the stone frame of the Sanctus bell can still be seen. The bell was removed in the 16th century.

 As we ride past this building today, we tend to take for granted the church with its stumpy tower, not giving thought to the people who donated funds ensuring we have a pleasing structure enhancing the view in the heart of the village. In the mid 19th century there was an extensive restoration to the entire building. There were sections stripped to the foundations and rebuilt using much of the original material as the poor state of those parts demanded. Parts of the old building could not be recovered which accounts for the 19th century appearance to parts of the church. The galleries were added at this time on the instructions of the Rev W. G. Townley. The church was subject to much enlargement in the 15th century, which included a four-light east window, angle buttress and the three lateral windows of the chancel, with cinquefoil (meaning five leaves) heads and rectangular tracery.

The window on the south side was removed to allow for a doorway. The vestry doorway with its four-centred head and continuous chamfer is also 15th century. The vestry has a three-light window on the north side with cinquefoils under a square head with a flat ceiling. The roof is of the hammer beam type with the 8 beautifully carved spread-winged angels looking down over the central building with 27 quarter-angels on the wall plates. On the south-facing wall there are 6 carved angels with intermediate smaller carvings. The north-facing wall is similar but has 5 angels.

The nave consists of six arches on the south and five on the north sides, they are two-cantered and are of two styles. An anomaly appears on the west wall when viewed from the aisle. The gothic style window above the entrance is offset from the apex of the roof. Dare I suggest the ornate hammer beam rafters were made on the floor and alterations to the south wall had to be made to accommodate installation, as account had not been taken of the offset? The cost of this outstanding craftsmanship would have been enormous and too great to alter. The outer walls of the nave have continuous mouldings while the inner has moulded capes and bases. The corbels on the arched stone of the west door are of Edward III (1327-1377) and his wife Philippa.

King Edward III   Queen Philippa

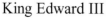

Pictures taken in 1980

The clerestory consists of two-light windows with cinquefoil heads under a square label. In the southeast corner of the nave is a stair turret, which rises above the roof and is crowned by a Sanctus-cote bell of ashlars (masonry that has been shaped) and the upper section of the turret is brick built with stone dressings. The lower doorway with four centred head is still there but is partly blocked, it used to open to the chancel. The west wall of the nave is 13th century with a modern buttress at the southwest side. The modern doorway is two-arched and is similar to the nave arches being of two types. The clerestory roof is of hammer beam with alternative tie beams and has queen posts, the hammer beams have quarter angels with outspread wings on a wall plate and the spandrels have pierced tracery.

The aisle windows are identical with three cinquefoil lights (5 arch designs) and trefoil tracery. The south doorway surrounded by stone mouldings has hooded grotesque heads at the ends. The porch has an outer arch of two types with moulded caps and bases and a hood mould terminating with masks. The inner doorway has four-centred arches, which are 13th century and the top stage 14th century. The west window in the lowest stage is of three trefoiled lights and two sexfoil widows above and is 14th century. The embattled parapet is brick built and dates from the 15th century with gargoyles at the angles. The font is 15th century and has an octagonal bowl with demi-angels holding blank shields on the sides. The shaft is a carved foliated canopy with flanking pinnacles and plain shields beneath. The faces on the font, some of which are now disfigured, were thought to be of Roman origin. All references to the Catholic Church were removed shortly after the reformation.

In the chancel is a brass triple canopy with the figure of a priest in alb. The alb is part of the rector's dress when performing his official duties e.g. weddings or baptisms. The inscription is missing but thought to commemorate William Mowbray, who was the Upwell Rector in 1412. Another brass of a priest without inscriptions is known to commemorate Henry John Martyn who was the rector of Yaxham in Norfolk in 1428.

There is also a brass plate engraved with a man and a woman kneeling at a desk with seven sons and four daughters commemorating Jane, wife of the infamous Sinolphus Bell Esq, son of Sir Edmund Bell's brother, Philip Bell of Beaupré Hall, who died in 26th February 1621.

> *"Here lyeth buried of whom may be sayd*
> *For parentage equall with most in this land*
> *No wyves, maydes, or widows more hartily pray'd,*
> *Than she in her closset, whose liberal hand,*
> *Was ever relieving the poor in their neede,*
> *For they and deseased of her did well speede.*
> *Her name was Jane Calthropp, as being a mayde*
> *Her mother of Rockwood of awncient descent.*
> *She married a Bell, and never delayed,*
> *By deeds and good usage to give him content.*
> *Children she had Eleven, whereof daughters four,*
> *Of whom remayne seven alive at this however".*

On the south wall facing the old rectory can be seen an ornate doorway that shows cross keys in the top arch which is the symbol of St. Peter. There are also inscriptions on wall plaques commemorating Ann Audley aged 24 who died in 1771 and her sister Lucy aged 38 who died in 1780, daughters of Thomas and Lucy Audley. This part of the church was extensively renovated in the mid 18th century, largely financed by Beaupré Bell. A stone giving thanks to him is set in the wall but is scarcely readable today. Also on this inside wall is a brass commemorating the Second William Gale Townley, Alexander Peregrine Townley and his son Major Richard Peyton Townley who was killed during the Second World War.

On the north wall there are plaques that acknowledge the work and of the Lee family who are mentioned elsewhere. There is also an intriguing canvas detailing charitable gifts from eminent gentlemen to the poor of Upwell from both Norfolk and the Isle.

This document has been written on skin and is in poor condition, it will not last in its present location indefinitely, consequently I think it important to record what is written. The text is written in "Old English" but recorded here in modern. Earlier I called the canvas intriguing because the first date on the script is 1562. Later, as you will see, there is mention of Pophams Eau. We know that Pophams Eau was dug in 1605 so it seems over 40 years had passed before this man's last request was honoured. There is also mention of the "adventurers" which was the name given to the people who put up the money to drain the Fens in the mid 17th century! The Old Bedford River was dug in 1637.

The benefactor list is as follows:
Thomas Lamb of Upwell be in his will of 1562 gave to the poor of this parish Norfolk and the Isle of Ely a measure of 3 acres in Plawfield Upwell to which was allotted by the "Adventurers" a parcel of land in Neatmoor abutting (next to) on Pophams Eau North. The rents are to be distributed by the churchwardens at Christmas.

John Fox by his will April 15th 1626 gave to the poor of Upwell in the Isle a house with 2 acres of land in the said Isle in Upwell abutting the river "Neen" south to which appertains a lot in Euxmoor abutting the 16 foot drain (The 16-foot drain is listed as being dug 1651). The rents are to be distributed on the Easter Monday. Also a house adjoining the Well Creek with a lot in Neatmoor near "Mumbrees" Drove rents of these to be for the repairs of this church.
There belongs also to the poor of Upwell 3 acres of land in or near Adcocks Hill in the high fen given to the Isle also 3 acres of land in a place called Shrewsnest Green abutting apon the Old River Neen given to the Isle.

John Boss gave by his will to the poor of Upwell the interest or the rent of the same to be distributed in bread yearly at the feast of St. Thomas.

Thomas Dixon 20th to the poor on both the Norfolk and Isle sides the rent to be distributed in money on Good Friday.

Mathew Batman gave by his will one fifth per annum out of his estate forever to be distributed amongst the poor in the Isle side in cloths at Christmas the whole estate in security for this.
John Bond and John Rapier, Church-wardens.

The eagle lectern is 14th century with a round moulded base supported on three lions. As with most monumental brasses the lectern is made from a soft alloy called "latten". Latten or Latton as it is sometimes called is a copper alloy of Copper, Zinc and Lead.

It is sometimes said that latten was used before the invention of brass but it is known the Romans worked with brass and English artefacts have been found that pre-date the 15th century. Lead was added to make the material more malleable and easier to form the delicate indentations seen on lecterns. This hollow eagle lectern is original and is an extremely rare type. Professor Banister Fletcher in his "History of Architecture" has dated it as 1380.

The plate includes a communion cup and a silver bowl which date from 1629 and a plate for receiving charity donations to the poor (alms dish) dated 1770 also of silver that is inscribed with the name Thomas Audley. Another alms plate dating from 1766 is inscribed "The gift from Francis Dixon 1767". There is a flagon of silver (1639) inscribed, "This flagon belongs to the Parish of Upwell".

The entire exterior displays ornate mouldings over the doors and windows finishing with carved images at the base of each. Many ramparts have been replaced or repaired but the pierced gargoyles have been retained.

There was further extensive restoration work carried out in 1836-37. Most of the interior was replaced with the exception of the nave and the north aisle roofs. The so-called "Free seats" in the middle of the nave were also replaced at this time along with the carved pulpit. Cost for this restoration work was £8,000 for which the late Rev. W. G. Townley contributed half. A brass plaque was fitted on the south wall giving full account of this restoration, which reads, "During the whole of these extensive repairs be it recorded to the credit of the respectable inhabitants of Upwell, that they forsook not the assembling of themselves on the Sabbath."

The church gates were erected when the churchyard and the surrounding wall were extended in the mid 19th century. They came from Peterborough Cathedral with vases on the stone piers from Wanstead House, Essex. The vases were replaced in the mid 20th century as they had badly decayed. A banner stretched between the delicate stonework caused the final destruction.

A local doctor's wife, Helen Barrowclough, financed the installation of the "pineapples" (as a symbol of hospitality) that replaced the vases and are in memory of her late husband, Dr. John Barrowclough, who practised in Upwell from 1923. There seems to be some confusion as some thought these mementos were actually acorns; however a short conversation with their son Michael Barrowclough confirms the former.

The existing clock was installed in 1864 replacing an earlier square clock that was set lower down and seen more as a diamond shape *(a picture showing the first church clock is shown later in the book)*. In the Upwell parish magazine of 1868 there shows a drawing of the St. Peters Church clock in its present location.

Trivia:
Outwell Church clock was installed in 1887 to commemorate Queen Victoria's Golden Jubilee.

In July 2005 the clock underwent a major overhaul and the drive mechanism was modified by having the most up to date mechanical direct drive to electronic synchronised motor fitted. Mike Tomlinson of William Potts and Son, Leeds carried out the installation.

Church Warden Tony Clingo August 2005.

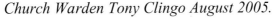

Mike Tomlinson of William Potts and Son, upgrading the church clock driving mechanism. The clock face was re-coated with gold leaf at this time. William Potts & Sons were based in Leeds.

Illustrating the clock driving mechanism 2005.

St Peter's church pre 1864 by Dr. John William Tubbs

The monumental tablets are few compared with many churches and most are relatively modern. The tablets on the south sidewall of the south aisle are placed in the memory of Ann the wife of John Huchesson, who died 17th June 1766, Hugh Wooll and his wife Frances 1845, Elizabeth, Mary and John Berry 1840 and William and Ann Hopkin.

Another memorial tablet commemorating local men who gave their lives in the 1939-45 conflict was unveiled in November 1950 by the Lord Lieutenant of Norfolk, Sir Edmund Bacon.

The memorial is made of black slate from Abergavenny Wales and is fixed at the east end of the south aisle near the brass plate commemorating the men who died in the First World War. The lettering was the work of Mr. David Kindersley and the dedication was by the Archdeacon of Wisbech and the Upwell Rector, Ven. S.J.A. Evans.

Mr. G.M. Holdrich of London built the original organ and it was purchased by subscription in 1868. It was sited adjacent to the west wall. For the technically minded it consisted of one row of manuals, the compass being from CC to F in alt and contains the following stops of pipes, 8ft. open diapason, 8ft. stopped diapason and clarabella, 4ft. principal, 3ft. twelfth, 2 ft. fifteenth, 10ft. bourdon, pedal pipes, two octaves and a third: german pedals, two octaves and a third, coupler pedal to keys, diocton throughout with its extra pipes, three composition pedals with double action to pull the stops out. The whole enclosed in a grand Venetian Swell. This instrument can be seen in St. Clements Church, Outwell.

The present day organ circa 1915 was made by Lewis and Co. Ltd. of London and is located in the Chancel.

This rare organ is now sited in St. Clements Church Outwell.

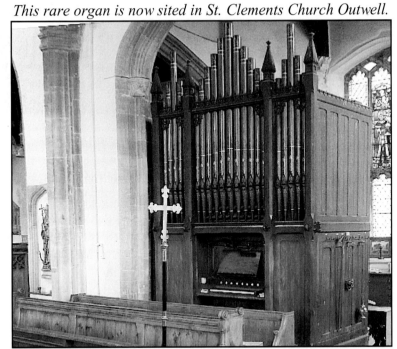

Trivia: *The church Registers begin from 1650 and are complete except for the years 1671 to 1703. The modern ablutions were added to the south wing 2011.*

LIST OF INCUMBENTS.

ANCIENT CHRISTIAN CHURCH

Robert de Gloucester ..,	1214
John de Offenham....	1260
John de Hadenham.....	1303
John de Sandale.......	1331
William de Stratton ..	1351
Peter Baker............	1374
Thomas Tyrington...	1396
William Mowbray...	1412
John Martyn.........	1428
John Harnham......	1446
John Ewbank......	1447
Thomas Cook, L.L.B	1466

Thomas Hutton, D.D.

Archdeacon of Bedford.	1493
Richard Skipton......	1494
Thomas Hobbys...	1497
John Harrys, B.D...	1505
Thomas Leson......	1517
John Badcocke......	1539

Patronage passed
to Edmund Beaupré Esq.

PROTESTANT   Single date: Start of term

Richard Barton	1562
Henry Bedingfield...	1567
Peter Fuller..............	1582

John Richardson, *Regius Professor*
of divinity in the University of
Cambridge and master of St. Peter's
and Trinity College...   1595

Thomas Reeve.........	1625
Nicodemus Parlett, B.A. ...	1662
Francis Goldwell M.A.	1666
Michael Griggs L.L.D...	1691

Talbot Hobart, *Presented by Beaupré*
Bell............   1698

Hugh James.............	1701
Bell. 1698. Hugh James...	1701
Timothy Rutter...	1740

Richard Walker, D.D., *Presented by*
Richard Greaves Townley Esq. 1765

Edward Pemberton......   1765

Jonathan Townley, M.A., *presented by*
Richard G. Townley Esq   1798

William Gale Townley M.A.	1812
*William Gale Townley M.A	1862

Presented by Charles Watson Townley
Esq.

John Beauvoir Dalison	1870
Alexander Perigin Townley	1908
Seriol Evans	1947- 1953
Anthony W G Cope	1954 - 1966
Richard Jeans	1966 - 1973
**James Martin (Temp)	1976-80
Raymond Wallis	1980 - 1985
Rodney Hacking	1985 - 1989
Thomas Heggs	1990 - 1994
Robin Blackall	1995 - 1999
Alan Jesson	1999 - 2012

*There were two different Rectors of the same name and of the same family from 1812 to 1862. They also appear to have had fathers with the same names!

**Canon Martin retired to a small cottage in Basin Road Outwell. In his retirement he was called upon to stand in at several churches.

❖   Rev Basil Davis came for a time after Rev Jeans and Dr Rake before Rev Heggs.

160

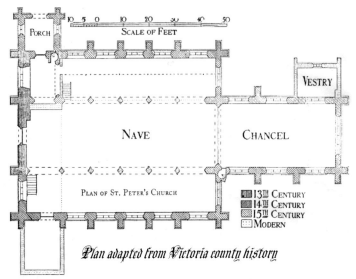

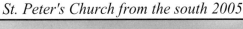

Plan adapted from Victoria county history

We are extremely fortunate as we enter the 21st century that the age of
demolition has passed. It is evident when visiting locations throughout
Fenland, that many old churches did not survive. Whatever we think of
their origins and the history surrounding these buildings they remain a
focal point that enhances our small villages and hopefully will forever
be preserved.

St. Peter's Church from the south 2005

Some past Rectors

Rev. John Beauvoir Dalison   1st Rev. William Gale Townley

Rev. Richard Jeans.   Rev. Alexander Peregrine Townley

St. Peter's Church choir in the 1930s.

Back row L/R: (standing)
Wilby Jarvis, Abe Mathews, William (Bill) Mathews, Mr. Gray, Jack Spikings, Stanley Johnson, Edward (Ted) Welfare, Wilf Allen, Will Mathews, Hugh Goodley, Fredrick Stevens, Hilary Russell, Arthur Brundish, Ben Webber, Charles Eworthy, Owen Agger, Bernard Rumbelow, Eric Henfry (church warden). Tony Clingo is currently the church warden.
Middle row: *Horace Overland, Eric Judd, Rev. A. P. Townley, Wolsey Rumbelow, ------ not known.*
Front row: *Albert Bentley, Stanley Canham, Eric Young, John Garner, Jim Blunt, Eric Overland and Peter Goodley.*

There was a very well attended Sunday school at St. Peter's organised by Pauline Jeans and Ann Frusher.

Pictured above:
Rev. Jeans, Mrs Pauline Jeans and the teacher Mrs Ann Frusher with the children belonging to the very popular St. Peter's Sunday school in 1969.

Listed below are just some of the children's names:
Joe Welfare, Paul Stittle, Andrew Hubbard, Jane Welfare, Gale Medlock, Vivian Goodley, Susan Winters, Elaine Calver, Susan Bays, Ann Lunn, Pat Thomas, Lesley Byton, Katherine Goodley, Mrs. Anne Frusher, Peter Medlock, Simon Bradley,. ...Brooks, Sheila Hines, Catherine Frusher, Debbie Hubbard, Richard Hewitt, Maloney Taylor, Victoria West, Susan Bowers, Kim Eggett, Juliet Lunn, Patricia Jeans, The Rumbelow twins, Robin Gray, James Brighty, Vivian Lunn, Sally Ann Petch, Steven Bays, Simon Gray, Rosalyn Frusher, Rachel Petch, Jane Rippon, Helen Rippon, Judith Taylor, Alan Goodley, Jonathon Bradley, Rachel Shepherd, Paula Rivett, Richard Jeans, Annett Lee.

ST. PETER'S CAMPANOLOGISTS

Pictured in 2007 are: Hazel Medlock, Pauline Wood, Graham Matless, Ian Ferris, Doreen Bainbridge, Norman Wood, Sylvia Short, Ted Skelton and Rev. Alan Jesson.

The church bell ringers although having a long tradition are usually heard but not seen and are normally overlooked when chronicles are written. I cannot recall reading anything about the ancient history of the Upwell bell ringers, which is not to say records do not exist.

The bell ringers are a much valued, integral part of St. Peter's. They meet up fortnightly for practice and are usually available when required with normal duties and special occasions. They made themselves available on one extra special occasion when they chimed in the new millennium.

In 1997 there was a national recruitment campaign to train thousands of new ringers in the art of bell ringing. The aim was to involve as many churches as possible across the country to ring in the new millennium.

In the St. Peter's ringing room on 1st January 2000 were: Tower Captain Doreen Bainbridge, Robin Mann, Sally Elmer, Jane Mitchell, John Medlock, Hazel Medlock, Sarah Reedman, Susan Baldam and Gordon Baldam. The present captain of the ringing room is Julia Neale.

Long serving church member Hazel Medlock demonstrates the training device used to help young church members with a desire to learn the skills of bell ringing.

The ringing room picture in 2012

There is a relatively modern record of previous bell ringers dating from the 1980s displayed in this room.

Much of what we know about our small villages today comes from the work done by William Dugdale, and a century later, the much acclaimed Rev. Francis Blomefield. His journal "Collectanea Cantabriensia" (collections relating to Cambridgeshire and other counties) was published in 1751. Francis Blomefield, a rural clergyman and scholar, has been described as Norfolk's greatest historian.

The Victoria history books of 1899 have included much of Rev Blomefield's work as can be seen in the following quotation from the book describing the Wisbech hundreds.

That mentioned below is validated by records held in the Norfolk & Norwich record office; it differs from a recent modern local publication. *A chapel or hermitage of St. Christopher was established in the high street of Outwell in 1348. No trace remains.*

In 1571 its site, then occupied by Edward Jenkyns, was granted to Richard Hill and Robert Don. According to Blomefield there was also a chapel in Upwell in the Middle Ages, dedicated to St. Botolph which was also granted to Hill and Don in 1571, when its ½-acre site was occupied by William Christen. The following year it was granted to Hill and William James.

William Watson mentions in his book "History of Wisbech": *An old house near the bridge, the last in the village on the road to Outwell, which had the appearance of formerly having been a chapel, and a roadway nearby called Pious Drove (now Pious Lane). This may be the chapel which, with two cottages, all in the tenure of the churchwardens, was in 1549 granted to William Warde. A guild of St. John in Upwell was dissolved in 1547; its hall was sold to Richard Hill and Robert Don in 1571 and re-granted to Hill and William James the following year. This guildhall was the meeting-place of the courts (sic) leet of the Bishop of Ely in 1648. Hill also received a close of pasture which had belonged to the chantry of Marmons in Upwell. A 'Guyldehall' in Welney was in 1550 sold to William Place and Nicholas Spakeman, and in 1568 to Hugh Counsaille and his heirs.* We have seen earlier it is not entirely clear where Thurlands Priory (Thirlings Grange) actually stood, could it have been near to the Pious Drove Town Street junction? George Smith, a respected local historian thought it could have been.

It is known at one time there were sixteen religious houses holding land in Welle. Undoubtedly those mentioned were included but much was lost during the dissolution of the monasteries and the disposal of other religious houses.

After this period the conventional church enjoyed more than two hundred and fifty years of being responsible for the spiritual interests of the populace.

In the beginning the first non-conformist "houses" were concealed from the hostile conventional church. I have said houses because that is exactly what they were. An early non-conformist house was sited at Small Lode adjacent to Bernard Morton's farm.

Henry Warby from Elm was an excellent local archaeologist, he carried out a dig in the back garden of this house and discovered a least three skeletons circa 1930. There was mentioned at the time something about Queen Anne's burial grounds but I have been unable to substantiate the report.

This house was used by the non-conformists in 1814

Baptist Chapel. Picture taken circa 1915

There was a much smaller Baptist church in the area of Dovecote Road before this church was built.

The old church building existed until quite recently.

The new Baptist Church was formed in 1840 and the building was erected in Town Street, later re-named School Road some four years later.

In 2001 there was mention of the Baptist Church being sold to allow it to be converted into a habitable dwelling.

A letter was sent to the Baptist Union Headquarters from the Fenland History Society in 2004, requesting permission to record the names of those buried in the graveyard. This was done and a CD containing the information is available from them.

On 15 March 2005, it was reported in the Fenland Citizen:

The old Baptist Church located at 159 School Road Upwell is soon to be turned into a dwelling. It is proposed to make alterations to the graveyard including re-locating or removing many headstones.

Although this church had been closed for services many years and the graveyard was not intensely attended, the news of its closure was strongly opposed by many.

All three WWII burials were exhumed and moved in 2008. Pilot officer George Hargrave, the son of George and Mabel Hargrave, died in a plane crash in September 1943, he was one of the last to be buried there. He was with the 57 Sqdn, Royal Air Force Volunteer Reserves.

Baptist Church, Upwell, Wisbech.

Church founded 7th February, 1840.
Chapel opened on 21st November, 1844, by the late Rev. W. H. Murch, D.D.

FORMER MINISTERS.

REV. C. MILLS	... Settled August, 1840 ...	... Resigned September, 1842
„ JAMES PORTER	„ October, 1842...	... „ July, 1851
„ E. GRIFFITHS	„ September, 1851	... „ April, 1855
„ JOSEPH BROWN	„ August, 1855 ...	... „ December, 1885
„ H. F. DEVALL....	„ April, 1886 ...	... „ September, 1887
„ A. C. BATTS ...	„ March, 1888 ...	... „ June, 1896
„ F. W. DUNSTER	„ July, 1896 ...	... „ December, 1897
„ F. H. RICHARDSON, A.T.S.	„ March, 1898 ...	... „ June, 1908
„ GEORGE SAGE...	„ September, 1908	... „ July, 1914
„ ROBERT MARTIN	„ February, 1915	... „ November, 1918

PRESENT MINISTER: **REV. THOMAS DOUGLAS**, Settled 28th May, 1919.

MANUAL FOR 1925.

THE CHAPEL.

MOTTO FOR THE YEAR:

" They helped every one his neighbour ; and every one said to his brother,
BE OF GOOD COURAGE."—Isaiah XLI, 6.

Above: Showing the original Wesleyan Methodist church near the Crescent. According to Victoria History of Cambridgeshire the building was erected 1826 and later altered to what is seen today circa 1900.

An interesting comparison can be made between the original church and the modern inhabited building seen above.

This is an interesting poster celebrating the first anniversary of the New Road Primitive Methodist Church.

First ANNIVERSARY of the
Primitive Methodist Sunday School,
UPWELL, NORFOLK.

On SUNDAY, the 21st of APRIL, 1839,

TWO SERMONS

will be Preached in behalf of the above Institution, by

Mr. B. DRAKE, of Snettisham.

Service to commence at 2 o'clock in the Afternoon and at 6 in the Evening.

Several PIECES will be delivered by the CHILDREN, and a COLLECTION made at the close of each Service.

HYMN I.

O THOU God of my salvation!
My Redeemer from all sin;
Mov'd by thy divine compassion,
Thou hast died my heart to win.
I will praise thee;
Where shall I thy praise begin?

Though unseen, I love the Saviour,
He hath brought salvation near;
Manifest his pard'ning favour,
And when Jesus doth appear,
Soul and body
Shall his glorious image bear.

While the angel-choirs are crying,
Glory to the great I AM!
I with them would still be vying;
Glory, glory to the Lamb!
O, how precious
Is the sound of Jesus's name.

Now I see with joy and wonder,
Whence the healing streams arose,
Angel minds are lost to ponder
Dying love's mysterious cause:
Yet the blessing
Down to all, to me it flows.

This has set my heart on fire,
Strongly glows the flame of love:
Higher mounts my soul and higher,
Struggles for its swift remove;
Then I'll praise thee
In a nobler strain above.

Angels now are hov'ring round us,
Unperceiv'd they mix the throng,
Wond'ring at the love that crown'd us,
Glad to join the holy song;
Hallelujah!
Love and praise to Christ belong.

HYMN II.

JESUS, see my pain and guilt;
Thou canst heal if thou wilt,
Say, "I will," and raise thy hand;
All shall flee at thy command.

Sin and sorrow, pain and fear,
All shall flee if thou draw near.
I believe,—assuage my grief,
Lord, and help my unbelief.

CONGREGATION.

May SUNDAY SCHOOLS increase around,
Till not a village shall be found
Where *men* and *children* are not taught
To mind Religion as they ought.

May pious TEACHERS multiply,
And young ones rise as old ones die,
Till steady Time his wheels shall stay,
And Death and Sin be done away!

☞ **The following day, MONDAY, April 22nd, a SERMON will be preached to the Children, at Two o'clock in the Afternoon and Six in the Evening, by E. WALLER; after that a PUBLIC TEA will be provided in the Chapel, for the Teachers and Friends.**

WATTS, PRINTER, WISBECH.

172

Picture includes: W.H. Hunter-Rowe, Mr & Mrs. W. Bridgefoot and Mr. Masters. At the New Road church in 1950.

A modern picture of the Primitive Methodist Church New Road built 1835-36. This Building was bought by Mr. Foti and destined to be the location for the production of the Norfolk Punch drink in the early 1980s. It is currently a domestic dwelling.

THE NEW METHODIST CHURCH

Mrs. W. Hunter-Rowe J.P. officially opened the new Upwell Methodist Church on Wednesday 26th September 1956 at a cost of £32,000. The organ was installed later, which increased the cost to around £40,000. Over 400 people attended the opening including many ministers and members of the church from a wide area. The opening heralded the end of a long fund raising effort headed by Ald. W.E. Hunter-Rowe who donated a substantial sum at the beginning of the concept and continued to give £2 for every £1 subscribed by others. The late Grace Hunter-Rowe bequeathed £15,000, £1,000 was received from the Chapel Department and further donations were from the Morton family. By July 1954 enough funds had been received to commence building this fine church, which was constructed on the site of the old Birdbeck House. A stone laying ceremony was held on Saturday 30th October attended by all the local officers and the main building contractor.

Laying the foundation bricks for the new Methodist Church 1954

Much of the superb Birdbeck gardens are retained with ancient pine trees, silver birch, beautiful lawns and flowerbeds superbly kept by the previous owner of the site, Ald. Hunter-Rowe.

Mr. T.F. Trower designed the church and the main building contractor was Mr. Harold Means.

He engaged many specialist subcontractors to manufacture and install the furnishings (J. Youngs of Norwich) and the stonework (A.J.Woods & Sons Norwich). In true Methodist style the church has a fine school room which of course was a requirement laid down by John Wesley more than 200 years ago and was one of the many endearing factors that made Methodism so popular. Over the years this building has been the venue for many organisations and has provided much needed facilities for the young people of the area, which was the wish of Mrs. Grace Hunter-Rowe at the very beginning. The footbridge opposite the church was constructed about a year after the opening of the church, greatly aided once again by the generosity of Hunter-Rowe family.

After the opening ceremony the congregation attended a memorial dedicatory service conducted by the Rev. Dr. W.E.R. Sangster assisted by the local Superintendent Minister at that time, Rev. A. Russell Potts.

The opening ceremony 26th September 1956

WATERWAYS

An ancient tale that mentions the village is the story of Lord Orford. He and his friends decided on a "Voyage around the fens" in 1774. He compiled a daily diary of his travels along most navigable waterways in the fens. Some historians have described his time on the water as "A wonderful voyage" and seem to hold him in high regard. When we read of his deeds today he can be perceived in a very different way that certainly would not be wonderful.

Lord Orford was known to have sold off a remarkable collection of paintings to the Empress of Russia. These paintings had been collected by his grandfather, Sir Robert Walpole, and were called the Houghton Gallery. He appeared rude and disrespectful to the fen folk he met during his trip. He was a man in an extremely privileged position and it seemed to me he was not long letting people know.
He assembled five sailing vessels, three tenders, a small ketch and three horses and started his journey near Lakenheath on the 17th of July 1774. By the end of the first day they had reached Salter's Lode.
To enable them to do this they travelled along the Little Ouse for just under twenty miles.
According to his journal he and his "Numerous friends" enjoyed themselves on the river, cuts, meres and fens. They dismantled bridges the boats could not pass under before continuing on their journey.
On day two they passed through Upwell and Outwell. A Mrs Turk, *this may have been Tuck,* of Outwell who received not one word of thanks, helped them considerably. After about two weeks they arrived at Whittlesea Mere and took part in races with Lord Sandwich.
They would have travelled through Outwell via the Well Creek and into the Old Nene at Marmount Priory lock. They passed through March before going on to Yaxley near Peterborough.
On the return journey they stopped at Salters Lode after again taking down the newly erected bridges. Although Lord Orford was accredited with his journal it was two "volunteers", Messer's. G. Farrington and T. Roberts that actually penned the work.
Mr. Roberts describes the people of Nordelph, Upwell, Outwell and March as "meanly clad and dirty", undoubtedly on the good "Lord's" instruction.

Mr. Farrington said "Outwell is equally remarkable for the ugliness of the inhabitants". This comment was echoed by Lord Orford adding, "Many very old women in Upwell, Outwell and March in general are extremely ugly". He did manage a few kind words for our "handsome" churches though. *The old cliché, "How to gain friends and influence people" springs to mind.*

After visiting his old family seat in Norfolk in an effort to find out more about this seemingly refined, educated gentleman, I came to the conclusion that he contributed little to man's knowledge of English history. Except he financed the building of a monument in the market place at Swaffham and sanctioned a journal that exposes the life of a 18th century gentleman of leisure. When King Cnut (Canute) travelled through Upwell on his way to Whittlesea Mere some 700 years before Lord Orford, he left a feature that is still there today. Often his ships suffered when passing over the wild waters of the mere, which caused him to have a cut made around it, giving birth to Kings Dyke, which is still recognised today. *This may in fact be conjecture but many believe it to be correct.*

It is known Cnut frequently visited the Eastern regions, it is recorded he visited the nuns of Ely to "hear the angels sing".

The big question is how did King Cnut, the all conquering king from Denmark manage to travel to Ely? Cnut was the king of England and later Denmark, *during the same period* (995 - 1035).

He travelled from Denmark across the North Sea, into the port of Wisbech and up the Wellstream. *There is some debate on when and how the name Wisbech evolved.*

Wisbech was a coastal town in the 11th century, with a persistent changing estuary due to the moving alluvium *(tidal silt)* deposits.

The Wellstream was the principal river of Wisbech at the time. *The principal river of Kings Lynn was the Nar.* The Wellstream carried the waters of: The Wissey, Lark, Western Ouse, The Little Ouse, *Medieval* Nene and the Cam (Granta), from Littleport to Wisbech before the 13th century. The Wellstream was in places, more than one mile wide in times of heavy rainfall. Its name came from the area known as Well (Welle), *the river of Welle.* The Domesday Book described all Welle as being Upwell, Outwell, Nordelph, Welney, Three Holes, Christchurch, Lakes End, Tips End and Euximoor.

The only remaining section and reference to this river is the tidal creek from Outwell to Nordelph, hence "Well Creek". The Wellstream also caught the water from the surrounding high ground before discharging into the sea at Wisbech. It was without doubt the most important waterway in the Norfolk and Cambridgeshire Fens, dating from before the Neolithic period. *The Great Fen Project has recently completed a 30 year study that validates the history of this and other old Fenland waterways.*

Just before the 13th century, the people of Littleport, being exasperated by the continual inundations caused by the outfall at Wisbech being choked with silt, diverted the waters of the Well Stream to Denver.

This once mighty river, being devoid of water it quickly deteriorated to become little more than a local ditch that swelled occasionally during the winter months.

Showing the area known as Welle, the heavy dotted line is illustrating the waterway alterations carried out by the people of Littleport. The dark shaded areas illustrate the high ground.

The Wellstream was being called the "Old Wellenee River" soon after the alterations to the waterways in the late 12th century.

Map showing the waterways after the "Littleport Chair" was dug to Southery, diverting the water of the earlier mentioned rivers to Denver.

Lord Chief Justice Popham's Eau cut through the Wellstream in 1606.

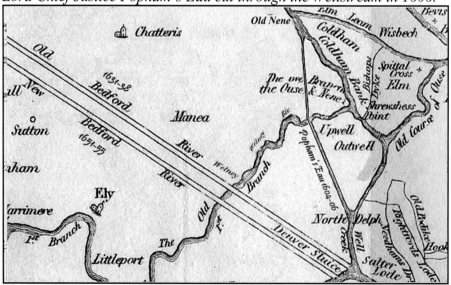

And the other 17th century drainage undertakings located south of Welney, cut through the Wellstream further starving the old waterway of water.

After the great floods in the Middle Level in 1841-2 and a desire to drain Whittlesea Mere, the Middle Level Main Drain was proposed in 1842. The man asked to draw up the plans to drain away the water of the 2,000 acres of Whittlesea Mere and to provide a central channel to assist drainage through the Bedford Level was James Walker. After suggesting three different routes and being rejected largely due to cost, a plan was devised using many of the existing waterways. The promoters of the Bill proposed a new cut eleven miles long, commencing at Upwell (Three Holes) and passing through Marshland into the Ouse, a little above Kings Lynn, by deepening the intermediate cuts and watercourses and adding smaller ones. Funds for the operation would be taxed at a level of 1s. 6d. per acre but no acre would be taxed higher than 2s.3d, except Whittlesea Mere and its reed shoals, about 2,000 acres. Almost all interested parties strongly objected to the new proposal as clearly indicated in the Statement of Opponents who came from Peterborough, Wisbech, Kings Lynn, Sutton, Mepal, Manea, Upwell and Outwell. Their fears were of being flooded by the new cut and the loss of land along the proposed route. A local vicar was quoted as saying, "The waters of Whittlesea Mere will come down and drown us all". The promoters overcame these protests and the Middle Level Bill, 1844, was passed. In 1848-52 the new drain was cut 12 miles long and 50 feet across the base. The prediction made by the local vicar during the proposal of the new drain almost became reality. In 1862 the river burst its banks and flooded one-sixth of the parish of Outwell rendering the surrounding land useless for more than three years. The cause of the breach near Lords Bridge was the collapse of the sluice at St. Germans under the tremendous pressure of the water from the Ouse. The cutting of the Middle Level Main Drain also severed the roddon of the Old Wellstream but by this time it was merely a small dyke with very little water passing through. From the end of the 17th century the vast area of land left by the decaying old Wellstream was gradually occupied by local farmers mainly for pasture. This may have introduced the word "Croft" into the area. Croft is an Old English word describing a "small farm" or "small-holding". The Wellstream roddon became known as the "The Old Croft" and later corrupted to the argumentative, Old Croft River. I have not seen the Croft River mentioned before 1830, by which time a river along this passage did not exist. Ordnance Survey (*maps)* tends to use local terminology regardless of exactitude.

An interesting conversation arose some years ago with a work colleague. Being aware of my involvement with local history he asked me to date a book he had in his possession. He said the book was about his great, great grandfather who helped to dig the Old Bedford River. I promptly informed him that his grandfather had to be a lot greater than that, and I would be pleased to read the book to try and ascertain its date.

As I opened it, the approximate date was immediately revealed as it was dedicated to Alexander Peckover, from the locally famous banking family. I was particularly excited when reading the first line of the book, "Work necessitated our move to Outwell".

The book was about a William Tolliday Streader, whose father was a navvy or "banker" as they were called. On reading through the book it became clear the family moved to Outwell about 1848.

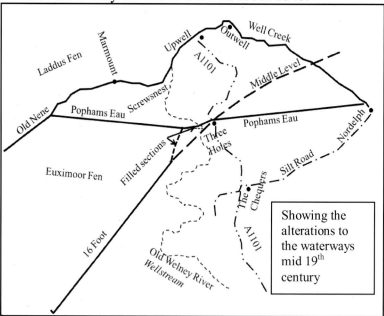

The Middle Level Main Drain was added on to the Sixteen Foot Drain and continued to St. German's. The section of the Sixteen Foot that previously joined Pophams Eau was filled, along with a small part of Pophams. Pophams Eau from the Nene joined the newly dug drain at Three Holes, and the flow of water in the stretch from Nordelph was reversed, relieving the Well Creek from much water.

The future of the Well Creek waterway was in doubt from this period.

William's father was employed to work on the new cut through Outwell, which could only be the Middle Level Main Drain. He was also a Methodist lay preacher and totally opposed to the demon alcohol, which caused many conflicts with the other navvies, always resulting in his becoming the victor.

One pay-day he refused to drink with the other men from the digging gang so they sought to pick a quarrel with him. He did all he could to avoid trouble but they continued to annoy him. At dinner-time, the persecution was renewed because they had mistaken his motives for refusing to fight. As the persecution continued he told them he was not interested in fighting and would rather help them than hurt them. But all this was in vain, they were determined to fight or drive him from his job. The custom was that the challenged party should sit with his "slop" (strap to assist with the barrow) over his shoulders and the man selected to fight for the rest should remove it.

The gauntlet having been taken up by one of his tormentors, a ring was formed round the contestants. Streader said, "Now my mates, I want to say I did not wish this fight but it is forced upon me, and I must defend myself". The fight did not last long for Streader as he floored the bully with the first blow and he did not seem to be in a hurry to renew the conflict. "I felt proud", said William, "in having such a man for my father".

William found a job as a horse boy, lugging the Fen Lighters along the local rivers. This presented him with his first act of bravery.

Fen Lighters working on the Old Nene at Upwell.

A boy named Church sank in the old river (probably the Well Creek) and would have drowned but young Streader dived in and successfully brought him ashore. William was 10 years of age. His father was a big man, this enabled him to be on the biggest barrow carrying a quarter ton and so earning the highest pay. William recalled walking to Kings Lynn to hear his father preach and then walking home late into the night. On one occasion, late at night, a travelling man at Terrington menaced them for money. William did not go into detail but said, "Our journey was not delayed many moments after father had helped him to his feet and made sure he was alright, we were on our way". William Streader obtained an education largely through self-study and partly through tuition from the Grammar School Headmaster in return for teaching Grammar School boys to swim in the Nene. He later became a Custom Officer at Kings Lynn and later at Shoreham before retiring to Acocks Green Birmingham and he is buried at Walthamstow. He had spent all his life around water. The book is entitled "To the Rescue, Being the life of William Tolliday Streader" who saved more lives (from drowning) than any man living.

At the age of 10 he came to live in Outwell, he worked on the Well Creek and the Old Nene at Upwell as a lighter boy.

His father was a navvy, employed to help dig, by hand, the Middle Level Main Drain

He was decorated more than thirty times for has acts of bravery.

William Tolliday Streader

Synopsis:
The waterway through the village of Upwell originally was a small section of the Well Stream from Shrewsnest Point, *Workhouse Lane,* to Outwell dating from before Neolithic times. The filling of the Wisbech Canal 1970, shortened the remnants of this waterway to what we now call the Boat Basin. *(The Lance Hunter-Rowe Boat Haven).* With the demise of this mighty river, the water from March to the Boat Basin took on the *(Medieval)* "Nene" name. The original Nene flowed much further north to discharge into the sea at Tydd St Giles. The Nene also carried the water of the Western Ouse *(West Water),* which joined the Nene near Benwick.
The Well Creek was originally a short tidal tributary off the Well Stream from Outwell to Nordelph. After the 13th century alterations at Littleport, it was extended to Salters Lode.
Today we consider the Well Creek to be from Marmont Priory Lock to Salters Lode Lock. The Well Creek comes under the remit of the Middle Level Drainage Board. The Well Creek Trust, formed in 1970, is a registered charity dedicated to opposing any attempt to close it and to keeping the waterway through our villages open.

The Old Nene through Church Bridge circa 1910

MEDICAL

Professional medical treatment was late coming to fen villages compared to the towns. One of the most common illnesses was ague, a crippling illness that was the curse of fen folk for hundreds of years. I suppose the nearest one could liken it to today would be malaria. Rheumatoid arthritis also plagued most adults and seemed to be expected as part of normal life. The vast majority of the inhabitants of Upwell and the surrounding area were land workers working extremely long hours. It would be common for women to work twelve hours a day alongside their husbands, harvesting the seasonal crops. When they returned home to their damp, cold "tied" *(rented from the farmer as part of their pay)* cottages often late into the night and racked in pain they would drink some "Godfreys Cordial". This was also given to the young children during teething time and to keep them quiet as they waited all day at the end of the fields for their parents to finish work. The working classes used this as a cure for all manner of ailments as pains were suppressed and a "feel good sensation" engrossed them. So what was this magical liquid that was the answer to all the medical issues affecting the labourers who could not afford proper treatment? It was a substance called "Laudanum". Laudanum was the name given to an "opium" mixture probably because it made the recipient happy, jovial and free from pain. Opium was grown all over the fens for hundreds of years; almost all farm labourers had a bed of white poppies in their gardens. Opium tea was the normal drink at "dockie time" (lunch break). This evil white poppy liquid was brewed up at night and drunk cold all day long. Opium pills were also readily available from the druggist and most general stores. A certain Charles Kinsley once wrote, "never a fen man's wife go by but what she calls in for halfpenneth of elevation to last her out the week, oh well, it keeps women folk quiet it do".

In the mid 19th century farm labours' pay was about 10 shillings (50p) a week and it was common to spend 1 shilling (5p) on opium. As this was a highly addictive drug dependency grew, so more was spent to satisfy the craving. The 1868 Pharmacy act prohibited small shops and traders from selling the drug, and control was gradually implemented. In 1893 there was a royal Commission on opium, which brought about its decline. By the beginning of the First Word War consumption had almost ceased.

Dr. Paul Millard researched the history of Upwell doctors and discovered a few more practitioners to add to my ensuing list. They included: Dr. Gill, 1744. Dr. Castell, 1786. Dr. Custance, 1791. Dr. Longmore, 1821. Dr. Wilkinson, 1831. Dr. S. Garrard, 1837.

Two doctors that became quite well known outside their medical duties were Dr Colvile and of course the renowned Dr. Tubbs.

Dr Colvile is listed in the Eau Brink Drainage Tax book 1818 to 1850 as being a farmer owning 70 acres in Outwell. His land was sited in Walsingham Fen near the Outwell Aqueduct where he owned forty six acres, and twenty four acres in Churchfield. A good living could be had from 15 acres in the mid 19th century so Dr Colvile must have been quite a man of substance.

Dr. Tubbs moved from Parson Drove to Outwell around 1850 then on to Upwell. He rented a room in the White Lion public house whilst securing the practice of Dr. Wilkinson. He later bought, under his daughter's name, "Lee House" in Town Street, where he lived up to his death in 1870. Dr. Tubbs was an extremely well qualified doctor and surgeon and he had also mastered the art of mesmerism (hypnosis) for which he became famous. He attracted eminent people from the area to witness his remarkable skills. Many were sceptical but he often did serious successful operations under close scrutiny, such as tooth extraction, leaving the patient feeling no pain.

Dr. Tubbs carried out one particular operation on the 26th of April 1854. Mrs. Flowerday, a gardener's wife from Upwell, was to have a breast removed by Dr. Tubbs under hypnosis. On the day of the operation committee members attended the London Messianic Infirmary to observe. Mrs Flowerday was put to sleep in four minutes, Dr. Tubbs sat down in front of her and made deep elliptical cuts down both sides of her diseased breast. The reports mention, "as the breast was removed there was surprisingly very little bleeding". On waking from her sleep Mrs. Flowerday said she felt well and that she had no idea the operation had been performed.

Dr. Tubbs was the Medical officer for the poor of Upwell and Outwell in the Wisbech Union. He was also the official doctor for the local Ancient Order of Oddfellows. He was a keen photographer; photography was the new technology at the time which caught his interest enabling him to produce tricks with his pictures that amused his friends. Dr. Tubbs' would have undoubtedly been more renowned had it not been for the invention of anaesthetics in the mid 19th century.

I had looked many times for Dr. Tubbs gravestone in St. Peters churchyard without success, there was much doubt as to where he was actually buried. In July 2004 a member of a working party from the Fenland Family History Society removed ivy and weeds from a relativity small unimposing grave to reveal Dr. Tubbs last resting place, ending the speculation. It was Mrs. Jenny Clingo, a member of the local family history group, who discovered the grave and recognised the name Tubbs as being an important part of Upwell's history. Inscriptions on the sides of the gravestone revealed he died 11th November 1870 aged 59. Other engravings on the grave are of his wife Elizabeth and his daughter Victoria who died April 26th 1859 aged 19.

17th October, 1870.

Monthly Register.

BAPTISMS.

UPWELL—24th November, Rose Sutton.

MARRIAGES.

UPWELL—3rd November, Frederic Barnes to Eliza Rumble; 4th, James Bellamy Dawson to Mary Elizabeth Egget; 10th, Frederick Hobourn to Sarah Wright; 11th, Leonard Hill to Ellen Hurst Lister; 18th William Brace to Sarah Johnson; 22nd Thomas Bellamy of Drayton, Nottinghamshire, to Eliza Turner; 25th, Matthew Britton to Jane Parker.

CHRISTCHURCH—27th October, James Lythen to Ann Gilbert; 4th November, James Hambelton to Eliza Ann Searl.

BURIALS.

UPWELL—10th November, Ann Rogers, aged 32 years; 11th Louisa Bennington, aged 66 years; 13th, Lætitia Mudd aged 29 years; 16th Henry Maycraft, aged 23 years; Francis Jackson, aged 86 years; 17th William John Tubbs, aged 59 years.

CHRISTCHURCH—31st October, Ann Gilbert, aged 2 years; 9th November, Phœbe Ann Roberts, aged 2 years.

Taken from the 1870 parish magazine

Other doctors practising in Upwell were Dr.Paley, 1873 to 1895. Dr. G.B. Sweeting, 1874 to 1908. Dr. H. P. Gilbert, 1890-93. Dr. B. E. Dalison, 1891. Dr. Dalison had important connections that enabled him to reside at the old rectory. His father was the Rev. John B. Dalison who was brother in law to Mr. Charles Townley (died 1893) and the Rev. Gale Townley.

The Townley family were undoubtedly the most prominent family in Upwell at one time. *(The Townley family is mentioned in more detail elsewhere in the book).*
It seems from 1875 to 1895 a number of doctors came to Upwell including Dr. D. Watson, 1893. Dr. J.F.Ollard. Dr. J.G. Gibbon, 1895-99. Dr. T. E. Price, 1895-1924. Dr. C.R Whitty, Dr. Marshall Hall, Dr. H Goodhall, Dr. Patchett. Dr. Parr. Dr. Jameson, 1897 and Dr. W. C. D. Hills, 1901. The chemist responsible for the pharmacy records from 1895 changed the style of recording the doctors and used only his initials so we do not know who Dr. P.L. was, only that he and Dr. T.J Walker were in practice from 1885 until about 1922, which probably would have been their entire working lives.
It seems Upwell has always been the preferred location for doctors in this region including a "Quack" called "Delvine" who caused most of the general public to turn against the qualified practitioners. Later Mr. Delvine moved to Outwell. This so called doctor claimed he could remove tumours without pain and leave no sign of his work. With his patients covered in a blanket or sheet he would place his hands under the cover and fumble about chanting weird noises. After a while he would suddenly pull out the "offending tumour," proclaiming "you are cured" and "you will survive". Unfortunately the rabbit or chicken, the genuine owner of the organ, was not so lucky! It was Dr. J.C. Burgess who was brave enough to confront the quack and expose him as a fake, thus restoring faith in the real doctors.
Dr. James Burgess came to Upwell from Hampshire in 1901 and lived at Lee House Town Street before moving to Lode house (Small Lode) in 1904. He came from a large family that were all connected to medicine in some way or other. He went on his round on horseback until 1914 when he bought his old "Ford Tin Lizzie". Dr. John Barrowclough joined him in 1923. Dr. Barrowclough retired in 1958 but continued with some of his old patients for some years. He died in May 1985 aged ninety-six. The whole Burgess family treated Dr. John Barrowclough with great respect, especially his daughter Helen, who married him on the 8th of July 1925.
It is interesting to note that Mrs. Barrowclough considered the family poor by modern standards as they only had a cook, a housemaid and a gardener. The gardener was Mr. Pears, father to the well-known Upwell

businessman Ron, and he was employed at Lode House for thirty years. There was a lady who came in one day a week to do the washing and a half-day to do the ironing and later a nursemaid. That demonstrates to us today how high the doctors were regarded in the early days of the National Health Service.

There were two other practices in the village at this time belonging to Dr. Price and Dr Hills followed by Dr. Fagan, the other doctor is not known. The doctors' stature today has changed considerably, largely because it has been rightly recognised that a doctor is just one very important link in the chain. Doctors today depend on other skilled workers such as electricians, mechanics, plumbers, electronic and computer engineers and such like, to enable them to perform their duties. Many people make up the chain today and are reliant on each other. *The Upwell Health Centre was one of the first practices in the area to become fully computerised in 1987.*

Dr Reynolds also lived and practised from Lee house in the mid 1930s. Patrick Floyd as a child remembers living in a small cottage next door to Lee house when Dr Reynolds lived there circa 1938.

I could find no official records of doctors over the years who have practised in Upwell so obviously it is difficult to mention them all. Other doctors who have worked in the area for any amount of time are as follows. Apologies for those I may have missed.

During the Second World War doctors were either elderly or from Ireland as they were not called up for service.

There were many locums in the village from time to time. Dr. McComas came in the 1930's and much later a Dr. Forsyth. A certain Dr. Rooney made his name in the village, as he liked to have a few drinks wherever he could find them. Another doctor was Dr. Hope. He was a "homeopath" who was at one time an opera singer and liked to stand at the bottom of his patient's bed and serenade them.

Dr. John Ferrie (1939-47) practiced at Beaupré Hall during the war; he also had a surgery at New Bridge. Unfortunately the war years took their toll on him and he retired soon after the end of the war. There was a Dr. Hawes in the village in the 1930's but little is known about him except he practised at the New Bridge surgery. Other doctors at this surgery were Dr. Dodds-Brown.

Dr. Dodds-Brown died in a car accident, when his car veered off the road into the sixteen-foot river near Bedlam Bridge, after visiting his wife in Addenbrookes Hospital. Dr. John Lightbody, Dr. Maurice Handol and Dr. Tony Rushmer (1960-1990). Dr. Cox, 1975. Some of those mentioned had joined Dr. Barrowclough at the Crescent Surgery. There was an announcement in the local newspaper in October 1977 which read, "The surgeries at Crescent House, Upwell will cease as from Saturday 29th October and recommence at Health Centre, Townley Close, Upwell on Monday 31st October 1977".

A superb brand-new purpose built health centre had been constructed on the old tram yard, bringing health care for the area right up to date. The doctors not recorded earlier are mainly those who have recently joined the practice. Dr D Brown 1976-78. Dr. D. Robinson 1978-82, Dr Millard 1982-2010, Dr. Bevan 1984 (due to retire 2013), Dr. Williams 1988 and Dr. Clarke 1990.

There have also been a few female doctors working in Upwell such as Dr. Pike, Dr. Marjorie Barr, Dr. Robinson, Dr. Blundell and Dr Jenny Haine. Some of the above mentioned doctors did part of their training at Upwell under Dr. P Williams.

Some doctors and staff soon after the opening of the health centre.

Included in the picture is: Dr Handol, Dr Millard and Dr Rushmer

Dr J W Ferrie   Dr J Barrowclough

The doctors of Upwell were supported by a pharmacy located at 16 Town Street up to circa 1891, later to become Ernie Johnson's shop. The original chemist at this location was Mr William Gouldin who was responsible for making up ointments, pills and medicine not only for the doctors but also for the veterinarys.

In 1865, 15 year old Thomas William Hill, the son of a Schoolmaster from Elm came to do his indentured apprenticeship under Mr. Gouldin. He later became a partner in the business. Nathanael and Ann Cragg who were drapers previously owned the shop that became the location of the pharmacy sometime between 1891 and 1901. On Mr Gouldin's retirement Mr. Hill became the owner. Ernest Loughlin M.P.S. was the main chemist up to 1922 after which time Mr. Hills' nephew Aubrey Hill continued under the Hill name. Mr Lawrence Hugh Floyd came to work for Aubrey Hill as the manager in that same year.

 Mr. Floyd purchased the business in 1947 and his son Patrick, who had assisted his father after leaving the RAF in 1948, took over the business in 1975. The dispensary then moved to The Crescent which was the location of the doctors surgery at that time.

Patrick continued working in the dispensary when the new Health Centre was built in 1977, which brought the doctors and dispensing under one roof. Patrick retired from the Health Centre in 1992 but continued with his part time job as a postman and working in the shop. Mr. Patrick Floyd took over the Small Lode postman's round from 1968 to 31st March 1993, succeeding Mr. Sidney (Bert) Stocks.

At the age of 66 Patrick decided it was time to close down his shop in October 1994, bringing to an end another chapter in Upwell's history.

Left:
Mr Lawrence Hugh Floyd at the Upwell Pharmacy. Circa 1950

A shop opposite church bridge, lately the Bridal shop, was a "druggist" and general store owned by Charles Chapmen Snr before becoming the post office in 1843.

Trivia: There were several "druggists" in Upwell before 1840. In 1815 an Act of Parliament was passed to regulate the manufacture of medications but almost any vendor could sell drugs to the general public up to the 1868 Pharmacy Act.

Only a few years before this date the local barber's shop might have been employed to carry out serious medical work.

William Gouldin's pharmacy adjacent to George Marsh Boot Maker

Above: Thomas Hill (in the apron). This shop is now the post office.

Nathanael and Ann Cragg's grocer and draper shop Circa 1880

Mr Patrick Floyd pictured in the Upwell Pharmacy.

Welle Pharmacy opened 1st Dec 2007. The first pharmacist was Ms Ning Wong who started Dec 2007 followed by Fazludeen Kamaludeen, the current Superintendant is Mr Chidi Nneji.

A brand new pharmacy was opened by Julie Garbutt chief executive of Norfolk Health at the Upwell Health Centre in July 2008, almost 130 years after the opening of the first one. The first practice manager was Mrs Rita Young followed by Mike Greenbank. Mr. Greenbank is also a partner in the practice.

DRINK

FOR

SPASMODIC AND FLATULENT COLIC OR GRIPES.

For Horses and other Cattle, give the whole in a pint of warm Ale or Gruel, and repeat half the quantity in three or four hours if relief is not obtained.

PREPARED AND SOLD BY

W. GOULDIN, Chemist and Druggist, UPWELL.

This is an example of a label that could be seen on William Gouldin's products which were sold circa 1860.

It seems the same product was suitable for man and beast!

Superb examples of the ornate labels, from the Patrick Floyd collection, that could be seen on the medication that was available from the Upwell pharmacy over the years.

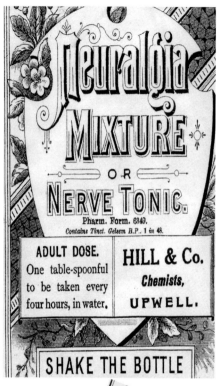

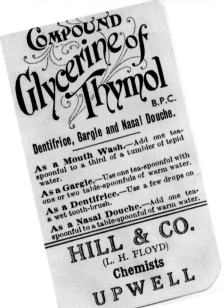

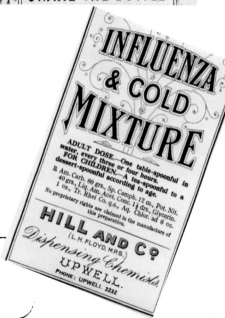

POST OFFICE

The earliest mention of a postal service in Upwell I can find features the Five Bells Public House circa 1840. It is likely this location was used before the 17th century. A report in the "Star in the East", an early Wisbech newspaper, makes some reference to the mail being unloaded at the Five Bells Posting House, Upwell. It is reasonable to assume Archway House in Town Street also was involved with the mail as other goods were delivered there. It is known the stagecoaches from King's Lynn to Ely swapped horses at Archway House. The remnants of the old stables are still located behind the house today.

A stagecoach approaching Archway House circa 1910

The Royal Mail can trace its history back to 1516, when Henry VIII established a "Master of the Posts", a post which eventually evolved into the Post Office.

In December 1839 the first substantial reform started when postage rates were revised by the "Uniform four-penny" Post. Changes took place when the Uniform Penny Post was introduced on 10 January 1840 whereby a single rate for delivery anywhere in Great Britain and Ireland was pre-paid by the sender. The more familiar Penny Black was available for use from 6 May the same year.

The first known modern post office in Upwell was located adjacent to the Queens Head public house, now part of The Bride Shop. Charles Chapman, the father of the man we have become familiar with through his local photographs, was appointed Upwell Postmaster 25 November 1843.

There was also another post office located near Bull Bridge that started business shortly after this date. This quaint old building still exists.

Bull Bridge Post office

Post office run by James Inman in 1893, after Robert Chapman.

Robert Chapman

Charles Chapman was also a druggist, draper and general dealer in addition to running the post office. His son Robert Chapmen continued the business from 1869 and until 1878.

James Henry Inman is listed as being the next postmaster at this location in 1881 and 1891.

The post office then moved to Bank House across the road into Norfolk as shown in the 1901 census. It is known this building was in the ownership of relatives of Charles Chapman at the time but the post office was run by James Henry Inman.

Post office next to Bank House.

By 1911 the post office moved to Oakley House next to Brian Tweed's butcher shop. It was to remain at this location until 1990.

It is unclear who the next postmaster was immediately after 1911. Suggestions have been made that it could have been William Cragg, Mr G. Davis could have followed him before the arrival of Mr. Harry Payne.

Harry Payne was at the Upwell post office for many years and involved himself with numerous activities within the village.

Harry was commissioned in the Great War and served in France. Just before he left he met and married Ida Andrew, of Murrow. He came home fortunately unscathed. His brothers stayed at home working on the land.

Harry was the more studious of the brothers and was an accomplished musician. He played the violin and piano and composed music for local performances by an orchestra he had formed.

Harry and his brothers were all Methodist lay preachers. They all took leading parts in the life of the villages, all well recorded in the local papers.

Harry moved to Upwell and the Post Office around 1940.

Harry's greatest work was as Chairman of the North Cambs Hospital for many years. He was also elected to the Isle of Ely County Council and subsequently became an Alderman. He was awarded the OBE for his work for the hospital and the community.

He later switched the C of E where he worshipped and preached at St Peter's Church, he also became the organist.

When Harry retired from the Post Office he moved to a house a few yards along the road and spent his time reading and painting. He died peacefully at home at the age of 98.

The Post Office moved to "Oakley House" in 1911 from Bank House. James Henry Inman was post master at both locations.

Harry Payne

The next postmaster was Marcus Roberts followed by Jean Tidmas.

Jean came to the post office 4th October 1974. She ran the post office for the next 23 years before retiring in April 1997. In a recent conversation with her she told me she loved every minute of it. Although, there was one evening in October 1990 she would rather forget.

Masked raiders brutally smashed their way in to the premises whilst Jean and her husband were asleep.

The perpetrators had overlooked the possibility of encountering opposition during their night shift activities.

Not to enter into too much detail the robbers were persuaded to leave the building after Jean's six-foot plus husband had a little word with them. They vacated the area much faster than they arrived.

The bad boys were caught the next day whilst attending the local hospital. During 1990 the post office was moved to its present location.

Mr Tidmas moved the Victorian post box to its present location.

Inset: Jean Tidmas

Pictured are the old and current Upwell post offices.

SCHOOLS

When I published the first Outwell book, I wanted to start at the very beginning of local structured education for the populace. The history books tell us the working classes were hideously discriminated against in so many ways. Looking back to the dark days, it seems inconceivable that the better off should be so cruel towards the very people whose toil kept them in splendour. What I wrote then is applicable to almost every rural community in the country and it is worth repeating some of it.

Not everyone welcomed the invention of the steam engine, after seeing George Stephenson's Rocket reach 30 miles per hour and trundling along on the Stockton and Darlington Railway in 1829. The complaints by some of the "very upper classes" were that it was a "deplorable idea and would encourage the working classes to travel". Compare that brilliant piece of English engineering to having a waterproof boot (Wellington) named after you! George Stephenson did not attend a school in the conventional way, being the son of a miner, he could not afford such luxuries. Stephenson gained an education through studying at night after a day's work as a fireman at the colliery. Similarly, education was looked on in the same way as travel. To educate the working classes was thought to be a dangerous idea and was not encouraged in the early 19th century. John Wesley, founder of the Methodist church with his brother Charles, was largely responsible for bringing education within the reach of common folk in Upwell and villages across the country in the late 18th century. He was the son of a Church of England rector and became a rector himself. He preached Christianity in a much simpler manner and held views that differed from the Church of England, so he was barred from the conventional church.

He travelled the entire country preaching and singing the songs written by his brother Charles. John Wesley died in 1791, leaving behind a movement that was about to sweep the country. By the mid 19th century a Wesleyan church could be seen in every village. Such was the power of Wesley's influences in the next 50 years. The members more than doubled, to reach the most remote corners of the land. If there were more than ten houses they would build a Methodist church.

The Methodist *"method"* was copied, and variations caused other similar churches to be built sometimes almost next door.

Sadly the decline of most of these churches was almost as swift. In the past 30 to 40 years they have amalgamated, closed, been left to crumble or have been converted for other uses. So what was it that made these churches so popular? One thing certainly helped, most of the Methodist churches had a (Sunday) school, a place where common folk could go and receive education, without the restraints of the conventional church and it was free. So what caused the decline? Could part of the reason be the introduction of National schools aided locally by a Church of England Rector?

Perhaps not, but the fact remains the first Methodist Church in the area was the Methodist Reformers church built in Nordelph (a hamlet of Upwell) in 1798 that had a free Sunday *school* which was open to all. A Wesleyan church was built in Town Street Upwell in 1814 giving free access to books which effectively was the first place for free education in Upwell. There were several small private schools including Archway House and what later became known as the "Parish Rooms".

Upwell's first public school, later called the Parish Rooms circa 1860 located in St. Peter's Road, almost opposite the old Wesleyan Church.

Around 1831 the Rev. W. G. Townley opened a school in Upwell *(Parish Rooms)* associated with the National Society. This school was attended by 217 children in 1846 and 250 in 1864. It quickly became apparent the school was unsuitable for the numbers needing schooling. It was necessary to set up a School Board for the combined parishes of Upwell Isle and Upwell Norfolk in 1874. The Board considered Townley's building unsatisfactory and in 1877-78 built a large new school for 304 children, at a cost, including two teachers' houses, of about £4,000. The old building was left with the Church authorities, who established an Institute and Literary Association in it.

Circa 1900

In 1909 the Upwell St. Peter's Board School was enlarged by Norfolk County Council, at a cost of about £1,500, to take up to 400 children. In the 1930s this school was practically full; there were 154 boys on the roll in 1935, in a department with 156 places. The situation, however, was eased when the secondary school was completed, and since 1939 St. Peter's School has been reorganized for 120 'junior mixed' and 120 infants.

St. Peters School mid 1930'S
L/R Back row. Gladys Warby, Mabel Goodger, Madge Payne, Hilda Forth, N/k.,N/k, Isobel King. Middle row: Elsie Young, Freda Hircock, Rose Day, Dolly Anderson, Blanch Atkins, Nancy Warby. Front row: Gwen Swann, Claire Elworthy, Mary Bridgefoot, Phyllis Rumble, Emily Dalton, Doris Brooks, Hilda Watkinson.

St. Peters School 1931
Picture includes: Mr. Walker (head master) – Hines, B. Hall, C. Copeman, - Carver, C. Gray, B. Forth, - Bristow, - Young, - Wenn, - Mathews, - Williams, - Forth, - Allen, - Burrows, - Warby, T. Forth, - Lister, - Lewis, - Brooks, - Horn, - Gay, - Towson, - Fiske, B. Brown, B. Gray, J. Carter.

A proposal for a secondary school at Upwell, to be provided by both County Councils, was made in 1931.

Owing to the economic crisis of that year, the Norfolk County Council withdrew, leaving the Isle to provide for its older children in the building planned for the Christchurch school. The scheme of 1931 was revived in 1934, but in a form that placed responsibility for provision solely upon Norfolk. A site was obtained in the following year. The school was planned for 140 senior children of each sex, and was opened in 1939. It cost nearly £23,000, including equipment. Additional accommodation in the shape of a Horse hut, for 80 children, was provided in 1948.

From 1951 this school took the older children from Emneth, Welney, and Nordelph as well as from Outwell and Upwell. After the Second World War, the school had over 350 pupils on the books at one time.

Central School Upwell circa 1955

The school became known as Upwell Secondary Modern, and near the end of its life, Upwell County Secondary School. It was the first secondary school in the country to have a swimming pool. Later the pool was covered and heated. R W Thomas and Norman Cousins both from Emneth, along with the Hunter Rowe family were generous benefactors towards the work.

205

Tom Cowling

Pictured are the remnants of the Upwell County Secondary School 1987. Below: A clipping showing the school pupils digging out the soil for the new swimming pool. The pool was largely paid for by donations from the pupils, staff and local benefactors.

B Dix

PRESS, WEDNESDAY, JUNE 18, 1958

Boys Dig Own Swimming Pool

Boys of Upwell Secondary Modern School are helping members of the staff to build a swimming pool in one of the enclosed quadrangles of the school. They are doing the work in their spare time, and some of the boys can be seen levelling the bottom of the 45 ft. by 25 ft. hole they have already dug for a local firm of builders to lay the concrete bottom.

Tom Cowling

The final parts of the school building being demolished in 1987

Children enjoying lunch in the main hall circa 1958.

This picture was taken circa 1955, along with many others, they are available from the Wisbech and Fenland Museum. The Upwell School class pictures were given to me by Mr J Frost who was a teacher at the school for many years. We have donated them to the Wisbech museum. There are approximately 200 prints relating to this school.

ODDFELLOWS

The Oddfellows organisation started in 1810. The Loyal Victoria Lodge Upwell No 3184, was founded in 1842 at the White Lion Inn, High Street, Upwell, where Benjamin Notson was the Host (Landlord). In 1844 it was recorded as having 24 members, rising to 49 by 1847, 96 in 1861.

From the will and Testament of Outwell Farmer William Reeve, the lodge was thriving in 1864, as it is mentioned:

"I also direct my said trustees during the life of my Son Royal Reuben to regularly keep up the weekly and other payments required to keep my Son Royal Reuben good on the books of the Royal Victoria Lodge of Oddfellows Upwell of which he is now a member and entitled to all the benefits of the said Society And such payments I charge on the said Twenty three houses dwelling house and land".

Quite why Mr Reeve was not a member of the Beaupré Lodge based in Outwell is not known.

By 1870, meetings had been moved to the Public Hall, Upwell, and the Secretary was James Webber Junior, Solicitor, of Upwell. The 1887 return showed that the Lodge had 369 members.

In 1897, membership had risen to 419, Samuel Mulley had taken over as Secretary and the Lodge had funds of £6,612.

From 1912, when the National Insurance Act was introduced, the Oddfellows became an Approved Society to administer National Insurance contributions and benefits on behalf of the government. This lasted until 1948 when the Ministry of Pensions & National Insurance (MPNI) took over this role.

In 1915, membership was recorded as 808. George Eggleton of Green Drove was Secretary, and funds had risen to £12,239.

In 1927, membership was recorded as 651 and funds £17,370, George Eggleton continuing as Secretary.

By 1939, meetings had moved to the Parish Room, membership was 642, funds £20,282 and G Eggleton was still Secretary but was replaced the following year (1940) by Thomas Bowers of Newfields, Emneth.

In 1957, the Secretary was Harry Payne of "Selbourne", Upwell, and membership was 452.

In 1966 the same Secretary remained and the meetings were held in the Village Hall, but membership had fallen to 333 and funds were £26,411.

In 1978, meetings had moved to the Five Bells Hotel, the Secretary was L W North of Tips End, Welney.

Membership was 302 and funds had increased to £30,109.

Les North d 24-12-09

By 1984, membership had reduced to 280, and financial administration of the branch was transferred to the Neptune Lodge No 10055 based in Wisbech. The Secretary of that Lodge, now renamed the Capital of the Fens District Branch is:

Mrs Alison J Adamson, Acacia House, 1 Kings Road, Wisbech.

LOYAL "VICTORIA" LODGE OF ODDFELLOWS, UPWELL,
ANNIVERSARY COMMITTEE, 1912.

Standing L/R: W Horn, A Russell, J A Wright, J Hill Cragg, A Calver, T Brown, R Simmons.
Sitting L/R: T B Lister, A Deptford, H W Hartley, S Mulley, (Secretary) J W Day, (Chairman) W W Jarvis, (Treasurer) H Overland, J Francis, W H Webber.

Trivia:
Oddfellow Magazine October 1883 Report of the 41st Anniversary Celebrations of the Victoria Lodge, Upwell.

"WISBEACH". Successful as was the resuscitated anniversary of the Victoria Lodge of Oddfellows at Upwell last year - a result mainly due to the presence of the Grand Master of the Unity - we are enabled to record a large meeting on July 27th, the occasion of the 41st celebration of the opening of the Lodge.

The arrangements for the day's proceedings were admirably made by the committee, and had their efforts but been rewarded by fine weather, the out-door affair would have been a most enjoyable one to all concerned ; but unfortunately the elements were not favourably disposed, and consequently the sports in the afternoon and the proceedings in the evening were rendered very uncomfortable. The brethren assembled outside the Public Hall at half-past ten in the morning, and walked in procession to St. Peter's Church, where the Rev. R. D. R. Cowan, curate, preached a very eloquent sermon. After the service the procession re-formed, and perambulated the chief parts of Upwell and the adjoining parish of Outwell, returning to the Public Hall shortly after two o'clock for dinner, which was presided over by the Rev. B. Dalison, M.A., of Upwell. Messrs. Pownall, Rust, and other gentlemen delivered suitable addresses. Having made some remarks on the elements that he considered a lodge should consist of to be successful, Lodge Secretary Mr. James Webber said that when he became their secretary some 25 years ago their funds were about £400. Now they had £4,000, and their liabilities were valued at £3,000, so that they had a surplus of £1,000. He believed that this balance was due in great measure to their resuscitated anniversaries, and to the good management of the affairs of the lodge."

In 1810, the Manchester Unity of Oddfellows became officially recognised by the Government. However, regarding Oddfellows social groups in England, the concept can be traced all the way back to 1066, making it one of the oldest friendly societies currently operating in the UK.

Oddfellows is one of the largest friendly societies in the UK having celebrated its 200th anniversary in 2010. Evolving from the medieval Trade Guilds, Oddfellows originally began in London in the late 17th century in a little different guise.

In 1810, the Manchester Unity of Oddfellows was formed by a number of local social groups joining together. Every year, thousands of people join Oddfellows, not just for the range of financial and practical benefits available but increasingly for the network of social events that membership offers and the opportunity for making friends.

To briefly describe why they are called Oddfellows: A group from many different trades decided to form a social club, collectively they were regarded "as a bunch of Odd fellows".

THE RECTORY

There was a Saxon church on the site of St. Peter's Rectory (now called "Welle Manor Hall") founded by St. Ethelreda in the 7th century. The site of the church was probably the most important historical site in the village as it was close to two waterways (the old Nene and Small Lode). At the turn of the 13th century King John allowed a market to be held near the site of the church and traders transported their goods by water to this market.

The waterways were the main means of travel in this area up to the late 17th century. The abbot of Ramsey increased the size of the original property in 1202 and used it as the headquarters for supervising the building of what were the first stages of St. Peter's Church.

The building at that time was a modest dwelling compared to that which exists today.

In the mid 15th century, the house was completely rebuilt by Thomas Cook and remained in the hands of Ramsey Abbey. William Mowbray resided at the rectory at this time (1412). At the Reformation, the property was taken over by the state and later sold to Nicholas de Beaupré in the late 15th century. The Beaupré family held land in Upwell and Outwell and can be traced back to William the Conqueror.

The relatively modern era started when Elizabeth Bell, daughter of Beaupré Bell married William Beaupré Bell Greaves of Fulbourn Manor. They were connected through marriage to Richard Townley from Belfield Hall of Lancaster.

Her grandson Richard Greaves Townley succeeded not only to Beaupré Hall but also Fulbourn Manor near Cambridge. The Townleys also held responsibility for St. Peter's Rectory. Charles W. Townley allowed his brother the Rev Gale Townley to live at the rectory until the mid 19th century. The Townley family was extremely influential in the area during this time as mentioned in other sections of this book. The Rev. John B. Dalison lived in the rectory from the mid 19th century; he was Mr. Townley's brother in law. He moved to Beaupré Hall while the renovations were being completed at the rectory from 1862 to 1870. The Rev Dalison died in 1916.

Part of the following description of the Rectory is transcribed from the work of Dr. A H V de Montgomery in 1940.

The old Rectory lies south of the Church, with which it is connected by a short path.

It is a large, lofty, high-gabled edifice of red brick and grey stone. Windows of the principal brick facade are rectangular, lead glassed and enhanced by grey stone facings. A prominent castle like wall with projected galleries separates those of the second and third storeys. Over these, which are crowned with rectangular moulded stone caps, rise high gables with rising battlements, and inset stone finials.

The long, high roof is of red tiles, chimney stacks are clustered and massive. Time has given the exterior a well-weathered, venerable appearance, which is enhanced in places by mossy patches, grassy tufts and encroaching ivy. While the eastern wing is a comparatively modern extension which has not too successfully conformed to the style of the main portion just described, the whole Parsonage is representative of Elizabethan domestic architecture of the best type. Hence we may date most of it back to the late sixteenth century.

Its entrance is most pleasing. One passes beneath a pointed stone arch of numerous moldings supported by rounded pilasters with neat capitals, all forming a reduced replica of a bay within the Church. Before him in the porch rises a massive oak door, richly carved in the Perpendicular style, displaying three shields and a heavy iron sanctuary ring.

Welcomed into the hall, a visitor finds it tastefully furnished in the baronial manner with old carved furniture, oil canvases, weapons and trophies of the chase.

Inside the Rectory as described in 1940.

On the left lies a large lofty room overlooking a part of the well-wooded garden: this is the library. Handsome bookcases contain some hundreds of volumes of different sizes, mainly on theology, many in rich, tooled gilt and glazed, old leather bindings.

Close by, one enters the drawing room, with its elegant furnishings and view over the lawn.

To the right of the hall is the dining room, not quite so spacious, but with dignified Georgian white enameled covered surrounding furniture "en suite." Its windows, one or two of which bear some intriguing diamond scratching from former days, look on to tall trees surrounding the churchyard. Leading hence is a small study.

Other apartments are decorated and furnished in a similar antique style. On the broad staircase is a particularly fine massive 16th century oak chest. It appears this chest took an unusual form, so much so Dr Montgomery listed it separately as being of special interest.

Towers.

Before the Rectory, and overlooking the churchyard, rise two interesting structures: old, lofty, battlemented red-brick towers pierced with narrow windows. Coeval probably with the dwelling, these constructions may well have envisaged three ends: (i) general defence in times of religious or social troubles; (ii) flanking towers of a massive gateway; (iii) quarters for watchmen against corpse-snatchers and graveyard robbers.

Many distinguished visitors have stayed within the hospitable walls of this extraordinary building, including bishops from neighbouring sees. The Rev. Alexander Peregrine Townley, born 3ʳᵈ March 1872 was the last Townley to reside at the house.

The Rev. Alexander Peregrine Townley died in 1947, his grave can be seen near the gate to the south of the church leading to the old rectory. His passing and the sale of all his household possessions on Friday 23 May 1947 heralded the end of an era. Archdeacon S.J.A. Evans resided at the rectory until June 1953 before moving to the deanery at Gloucester.

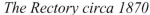

The Rectory circa 1870

The designed purpose for this grand old building that is steeped in history, ended in the mid 1970s when it was considered too costly to maintain. It was sold to a Norfolk businessman, Mr Branson, and renamed Sanford House.

Mr Branson later sold the Rectory to Mr Eric St.John-Foti who renamed the house Welle Manor Hall.

THE UPWELL TRAM

There have been at least five books written on the Wisbech to Upwell tramway so finding material that has not been seen is extremely difficult.

Nevertheless I feel I have to mention the old tram as it was an integral part of the village from 1884 to 1966. After extending the track from Outwell, the plans were to take it through to Three Holes and on to Welney but as we know that did not happen.

The land used to accommodate the tram-yard circa 1883 was bought from Charles Chapman of Walnut House.

Some of the old timers have told me it was not unusual to see queues of horse and carts along New Road, waiting to off-load products grown on the land. Strawberries were being loaded on the tram trucks right up to the time of closure.

This picture illustrates the entrance into the tram yard from New Road.

The above picture was taken by John Francis in 1960.
Bill Williamson was the manager of Coote and Warren coal merchants, they conducted their business from the tram yard.

Coote and Warren coal-lorries returning to the tram yard.

The station foreman at the time of closure in 1966 was Eric (Mike) Francis

J Francis

1960

The Upwell Health Centre is currently located on this site.

Pictured are Mr Hills and Mr Peacock with the steam tram that later inspired Rev Awdry to write the Toby the Tram books. Toby still features in the Thomas the Tank stories

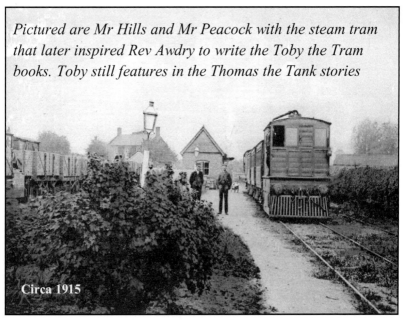

Circa 1915

Mr. Hill was the chemist and Mr Leslie Peacock Station Foreman.

*Wife of the coal merchant's manager, Mary Williamson saying goodbye
to the guard Tim Downs, as the last Upwell tram leaves the village.*

Bill Williamson col

My gratitude goes to Bill & Mary Williamson for having the
forethought to record this event. We are honoured to have
these previously unpublished pictures.

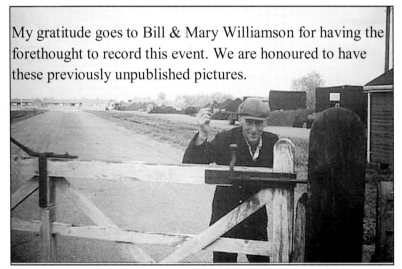

Mike Francis closing the Upwell tram-yard gate for the final time.

The official date of closure was 23 May 1966, the last tram departed
from Upwell tram-yard at 3-30pm on Friday 20 May 1966.
The tram had been operating for just over eighty two years.

THEY ARE REMEMBERED

When I wrote the book "Outwell in a Nutshell", I did much soul searching as I couldn't decide if it was right to record the sad incidents that have occurred in the villages over the years. Following many conversations with the people close to these events and listening to their views it became clear to me that the vast majority of them were happy to have their loved ones remembered in this way. Many young lives have been cut short which means the villages have suffered sad losses that have unfortunately become part of our history. It was decided in this book we will record only those lost in the two world wars. There will be later, individual tributes but for now, the following should and will always be remembered in the village of Upwell.

There were around sixty young Upwell men who lost their lives during the Great War. It is not absolutely clear if all names of those lost are actually inscribed on the monument erected in 1920. A beautiful hand written list of those fallen was found in a shed recently, which differs from the names on the official list. The following is as they are listed.

First World War (1914-1918)

John Cawthorn Allen (Green Drove), Donald W. Amps (Lord Nelson, Lakesend), Walter Baines (Town Street), Samuel F. Belderson (Wisbech Road, Outwell), Thomas Bowers, John Bowles, Stanley Canham (Town Street), Herbert Cole (Prospect House, Pious Drove), George William Cox, Thomas Davis, Arthur Deighton, Arthur Dunham (Marmont Priory Sluice), George Feetham, Herbert Feetham, Hubert Hardiment (Pingle Bridge), George William Hartley (Lotts Bridge), Edward Haycock (Small Lode), Albert Edward Hills (Small Lode), Sidney Hills, Charles William Hovell, Walter Jermey (Council Houses, Three Holes), Charles Johnson, George Stewart Johnson (bakers's son – Town Street), Hugh Johnson, Leonard Johnson, Robert Lindsay, Percy Palmer, Arthur Pleasants, James Herbert Pollington, John Henry Pollington, George Pratt (fruit grower -Town Street), Sidney Pratt (brother of George), Thomas Punter (Small Lode), Frank Punter (62 St. Peter's Road), Percy Rogers, Arthur Roofe, Alfred Russell (Lilybank, Upwell), George Rust, Fred (William) Sandal (Thurlands Drove), George Sandal, Herbert Shepherd, Elijah Skeels, Bert Smith (The Dovecot), Sidney Smith (brother of Bert), Josiah Steward (March Riverside), Horace Stone, Walter Henry Taylor,

Fredrick William Towson, Fredrick Trower (Town Street), Walter Vurley (Church Bridge), Herbert Wakefield (The Horse Head, Three Holes), Joseph Percival Warby, William Reginald Warby, George Edward Ward (March Riverside), Arthur Wenn (Workhouse Lane), Walter F. Woolner (Hundreds Farm, Welney) and Henry Youngs. George and Herbert Feetham are also mentioned on the Outwell memorial.

Not on the memorial, but listed elsewhere:-

Ben Thorn, Isaac Russell, John Cooper died on service 1918, Percy A Newell died while serving with Y.M.C.A. January 1915, George William Smith (Three Holes), John F. West died in hospital in 1920 as a result of the conflict.

Second World War (1939- 1945)

Douglas Gooch L/Cpl Grenadier Guards (husband of Dorothy), killed 8-11-1945 aged 25 (Buried in Cassiono War Cemetery Italy), George Melton Hargrave Pilot Officer (57 Squadron RAF volunteer reserve flying Lancaster Bombers), died 28-9-1943, John David Nunn (Royal Navy - HMS Collingwood), died 18-6-1943, Charles Derek Ward Sgt (106 Squadron RAF Volunteer Reserve - Lancasters) died 15-10-42, lived at Lister's Drove, Ernest Watson, Jack (Dennis) Young (son of William & Rachel) died 3-7-1945 whilst POW aged 26, Stanley Parmenter, Harry Plumb, Cpl. 4th Suffolk Regiment, (son of Arthur & Lucy of Town Street) died 11-12-1943 aged 30, Richard Townley Major (son of Rev. Alexander Peregrine Townley MA from the Upwell Rectory) died 9-5-1945, Jack Wooll. Alfred Arnold lived at Small Lode Upwell but he is listed on the Outwell memorial.

Some of the above mentioned were born in places other than Upwell, but lived there when called for service, others were born in Upwell and are mentioned on other memorials. Consequently confusion with the listing was inevitable.

Upwell paid dearly during these two World Wars.
The families and the village gave so much.

It was a high price to pay and they are remembered.

There are so many topics we have not been able to publish this time but hope to do so in the future. We are living in difficult times and spare cash is hard to find. History books are not a priority for many. We have tried to produce this book at a price that is viable to all and will encourage us to do more.

Future topics:

The History of the cinema, Victorian shops, The Brass band,

The Olde Mill, More on the waterways, Modern commerce,

Birdbeck House, *although Birdbeck, an ancient area in "Upwell", is commemorated in "Outwell"!*

The Upwell fire engine, More on Upwell people, the trades and tradesmen, more stories such as the "Whales Jawbone".

The Gas works, the war years and more on the tram.